D. Caroline Coi

American Eskimo Dogs

Everything about Purchase, Care, Nutrition,
Breeding, Behavior, and Training

With 51 Color Photographs
Illustrations by Michele Earle-Bridges

BARRON'S

About the Author

Caroline Coile is an award-winning author who has written articles about dogs for both scientific and lay publications. She holds a Ph.D. in the field of neuroscience and behavior, with special interests in canine sensory systems, genetics, and behavior. Her own dogs have been nationally ranked in conformation, obedience, and field-trial competition.

All inquiries should be addressed to
Barron's Educational Series, Inc.
250 Wireless Boulevard
Hauppauge, NY 11788

International Standard Book No. 0-8120-9198-1

Library of Congress Catalog Card No. 95-7319

Library of Congress Cataloging-in-Publication Data
Coile, D. Caroline.
    American Eskimo dogs: everything about
purchase, care, nutrition, breeding, behavior,
and training/D. Caroline Coile; drawings by
Michele Earle-Bridges.
        p. cm.—(A complete pet owner's manual)
    Includes bibliographical references (p. 112)
    and index.
    ISBN 0–8120–9198–1
    1. American Eskimo dog. I. Title. II. Series.
SF429.A69C65   1995   95-7319
636.7′3—dc20   CIP

Printed in Hong Kong

678   9955   987654

Acknowledgments

The information contained in this book comes from a variety of sources: breeders, original research, scientific articles, veterinary journals, and a library of dog books. But by far my most heartfelt gratitude must go to my most demanding teachers, who have taught me the skills of both home repair and dog repair, allowed ample testing opportunities for behavioral problem cures, and whetted my curiosity (and carpets) about everything canine for the past 20 years: Baha, Khyber, Tundra, Kara, Hypatia, Savannah, Sissy, Dixie, Bobby, Kitty, Jeepers, Bean-Boy, Junior, KhaKha, Wolfman, and Stinky.

Photo Credits

Susan Green: cover, pages 4, 36, 55, 58, 59, 68, 73, 77, 92, 97, 101, 104, inside back cover, back cover; Debbie McIntyre: pages 9 top, 16, 96; Kimberlee Herzog: inside front cover, pages 5, 30, 50, 51, 54, 62, top and bottom; Theresa Wright: pages 8, 105; Ellen Parkin: pages 9 bottom, 12, 18, 23, 27, 33, 76, 80, 85, 88, 100; Patrea L. Pabst: pages 13, 41, 72, 84; Jan VanHorn: pages 19, 22, 26, 48; D. Caroline Coile: pages 31, 40, 81, 89; Barbara Capps: page 63; Talitha M. Bell: page 69; Judith E. Strom: page 108.

Important Notes

This pet owner's guide tells the reader how to buy and care for an American Eskimo dog. The author and the publisher consider it important to point out that the advice given in the book is meant primarily for normally developed puppies from a good breeder—that is, dogs of excellent physical health and good character.

Anyone who adopts a fully grown dog should be aware that the animal has already formed its basic impressions of human beings. The new owner should watch the animal carefully, including its behavior toward humans, and should meet the previous owner. If the dog comes from a shelter, it may be possible to get some information on the dog's background and peculiarities there. There are dogs that, as a result of bad experiences with humans, behave in an unnatural manner or may even bite. Only people that have experience with dogs should take in such animals.

Caution is further advised in the association of children with dogs, in meeting with other dogs, and in exercising the dog without a leash.

Even well-behaved and carefully supervised dogs sometimes do damage to someone else's property or cause accidents. It is therefore in the owner's interest to be adequately insured against such eventualities, and we strongly urge all dog owners to purchase a liability policy that covers their dog.

Contents

Preface

The enigmatic Eskie—a breed both rare and familiar, ancient and modern—is a breed of such undeniable appeal that its cuteness has been described as its major flaw. Circus dog, farm dog, watchdog, even draft dog—the American Eskimo dog's original role is not clear. But one thing never disputed is that the American Eskimo dog ("Eskie" to its friends) is a companion dog par excellence.

Look in the classifieds of most newspapers and you can find an advertisement for a litter of Eskies, although often incorrectly identified as Eskimo spitz dogs, or simply spitz. Eskies are popular pets. Where then is the rich source of breed information so readily available for other popular breeds? In many ways the Eskimo dog—a breed that many of us met in our childhood—is just stepping into the limelight of modern breed recognition. It is a breed with a rich heritage, but a heritage in danger of being lost. As the Eskie enters a new era, breeders face a new challenge: that of preserving this spunky little dog, which has already proven its mettle in a variety of roles, while promoting it in a world of show dogs that far too often rewards extremes. And the Eskie is not a dog of extremes—its very moderation has been what has enabled it to be an all-American dog.

In the following chapters you will meet the Eskie and explore it's history. Perhaps you may even decide to be a part of its future.

D. Caroline Coile, Ph.D.

The American Eskimo Dog is one of the newest faces on the AKC scene.

Understanding the American Eskimo Dog

One of the newest faces on the American Kennel Club (AKC) scene is that of the American Eskimo dog. And though this merry dog is no newcomer in American homes, many people are just now discovering one of America's best kept canine secrets. That a breed of such charm and appeal should only now gain the recognition it has long deserved is just one chapter in the checkered past of this little white tornado.

Breeds of dogs are broadly categorized as those originated to hunt, those originated to work, and those originated as lap dogs. Although the American Eskimo dog will gladly give chase to marauding squirrels, will gleefully give its best at pulling a sled, and will ball up on any family member's lap without hesitation, it is a breed whose popularity cannot be traced to only one role. Though documentation about the breed's origins is obscure, it is known that the American Eskimo dog is a modern variation of a very ancient family of dogs.

The Eskie's Past

That ancient family is the spitz family, a group of dogs that still possess many wolflike characteristics: erect pointed ears, double coats, and moderation in body proportions. Most of this family (also called the northern or Nordic breeds) flourished in cold and unforgiving environments, and served man in a variety of functions that required courage, strength, intelligence, and determination.

In the harsh northern world, there was little patience for a dog that could not pull its weight (actually, in the case of sled dogs, pull many times its weight). Thus there was rigorous selection for a hardy, hardworking dog that could serve as a draft animal, hunting companion, and watchdog. These traits have continued to make this family popular today, but also have served to make many of them difficult to handle for the average dog owner. Breeds such as the Alaskan malamute, Siberian husky, Samoyed, chow chow, keeshond, Pomeranian, and American Eskimo dog descend from this strong-willed group of dogs.

Although simply called a "spitz" more often than any of the other spitz breeds in America, the American Eskimo dog is in many ways not the prototypic spitz. While still retaining the tenacious spirit and can-do attitude of its ancestors, the Eskie's most important role is now that of family pet. Too small to perform many of the tasks required of its forefathers, it nonetheless is the modern-day answer to the jack-of-all-trades dog: vocal watchdog, lively helpmate, and affectionate companion. So how did this little dog evolve?

As many of the spitz breeds fanned throughout Europe, different areas developed distinct subgroups of spitz dogs, which eventually became distinguished by their place of origin. The most well documented of these is the German spitz, which was bred in five separate size classifications, each having within it separate lines based upon color. Today's keeshond and Pomeranian descend at least in part from two of these varieties. The Eskie probably descends from several varieties of the German spitz, in addition to some more recent influence from the keeshond and the Pomeranian. In each of these size varieties there existed pure white strains of dogs. In addition, the Italian spitz (Volpino Italiano), a small, white dog similar to today's Eskies, almost certainly was incorporated into the breeding pool.

With the keeshond and Pomeranian becoming established in Britain, and then America, their breed fanciers drafted standards to describe the desired breed features. In part, the Eskimo dog owes its existence to the exclusion of dogs resembling it from the standards of the keeshond and Pomeranian. Although the keeshond originally came in several colors, including white, when the British and Americans chose to accept only the gray color, the white dogs of this breed were suddenly excluded from recognition. And although the often white Pomeranian was originally recognized in two size varieties, when the larger (over 8 pounds [3.6 Kg]) variety was dropped, these dogs, too, were without breed recognition. Thus, in the early part of the twentieth century there were two groups of related purebred dogs, both somehow excluded from the recognition due them, and both with considerable numbers. Lacking official breed status, and without an organized breed club, the fate of these dogs has become obscured with time.

The Spitz Becomes American

Although these were far from banner years in the show ring for these small white spitz dogs, something more important was happening on the home front. Undaunted by the lack of

Eskies in the circus in the early 1900s gained many admirers with acts such as this.

such formalities as kennel club recognition, owners of these versatile dogs continued to cherish them. European emigrants to America brought with them their most valued possessions, among them their German spitz dogs. The little white spitz dogs flourished and were quick to adopt America as their own. In fact, it was short order before they came to be commonly called the American spitz.

The American spitz soon found its way into Americana through another route: the circus. In the early 1920s, these dazzling daredevils were a favorite circus attraction—performing tricks to music, in acts with clowns or ponies, wire walking, and even weaving in and out of moving wagon wheel spokes and horses' hooves. One of the most striking acts was the all-white statue act, where white dogs, white horses, and white painted and cos-

Eskies are good at hunting, working, and sitting on laps, and they are also good with children, as long as the children are taught how to be good with them. This young owner and her two miniatures display mutual affection and respect.

tumed humans would perform different tricks, freezing in various poses at intervals so that they appeared to be one large intricate marble statue. With their dazzling white coats, obvious good humor, quick intelligence, and uncanny abilities, is it any wonder that many early circus-going families left with a vision of an Eskie as their next dog? And in fact, there were often puppies available from the circus, so that wherever the circus traveled, a small but influential trail of Eskies and Eskie admirers remained. With the illustrious heritage of famous circus dogs, new owners were eager to record the performing dogs in their dog's backgrounds, complete with information about tricks performed and the circus with which they performed. To this day, many Eskie pedigrees

can be traced back to these famous working circus dogs.

UKC Recognition

The registry of purebred dogs for show purposes in the United States has been dominated by the American Kennel Club (AKC). Although not invited into the auspices of AKC recognition, the American spitz was recognized as a breed by the other principle registry, the United Kennel Club (UKC). The two kennel clubs differed in a fundamental manner in the requirement for registering an individual dog as purebred. The AKC was then and is now primarily a pedigree-based registry; it required that a certain number of generations of a dog's ancestry be documented and recorded with some AKC-recognized registering

The variation in sizes makes the Eskie an especially versatile breed. A miniature and a standard are shown here.

body before according it registration. The UKC's emphasis was upon hunting and working ability, and as such put more value upon the individual dog than the dog's background. In recognition of the fact that many purebred dogs existed without documented pedigrees, they allowed individuals to be single-registered as a particular breed as long as sufficient evidence was submitted that a dog was typical for its breed. In order to encourage purity of ancestry, the UKC awards the Purple Ribbon (P.R.) title to dogs that have seven generations of ancestors registered with the UKC. The allowance of single-registration was a boon to the American spitz, because the breed enjoyed a grassroots popularity, still with little emphasis upon fancy pedigrees and show dogs.

One last change was made to send the American spitz on its way as a

This "dog of the people" is now also becoming a popular contender at dog shows.

household name—and that was a name change. In the wake of World War I, with anti-German sentiment strong, the Germanic spitz was replaced by the more American Eskimo, so the breed became known as the American Eskimo (not to be confused with the breed Eskimo dog, which was a much larger sled dog).

The combination of the circus performers and word of mouth continued to make the American Eskimo a "dog of the people." Most new Eskie owners did not choose their breed from a book, but fell in love with their neighbor's wonderful white dog and had to have one just like it. Dogs were single-registered with UKC, but only a handful of diligent breeders methodically registered all of their stock. For many years there was no breed standard, no breed club, and no breed shows, so that registration entitled owners to limited opportunities compared to other breeds. Although a prototypic breed standard was advanced in the late 1950s, it was not until 1970 that the standard was officially adopted, the first show for Eskies was held, and the National American Eskimo Dog Association (NAEDA) was founded. At that time NAEDA made an important decision that would forever change the Eskie's place in dogdom: the UKC would no longer accept single-registrations for Eskies. They realized that the effect of the single-registration policy was to promote a suspicion among the public that the American Eskimo was not of pure breeding. As long as single-registration was allowed, there was the possibility that a dog could be registered as an Eskie that happened to be a lucky mix. And as long as this was a possibility, the American Eskimo could never hope to gain recognition from kennel clubs (such as the AKC) that based registration on pedigree documentation.

Because of this decision, the Eskie has gained the respect from the dog world that it so richly deserved. Now Champion and Grand Champion Eskies grace Purple Ribbon pedigrees. In fact, because single-registration has been closed since 1970, enough generations have passed so that almost all present-day Eskies carry the P.R. title as a matter of course.

AKC Recognition

But even though single-registration no longer stood in the way of AKC recognition, the AKC requirement of submitting the breed's UKC studbook for inspection could not be complied with by the UKC. Instead, another national breed club was formed, the American Eskimo Dog Club of America (AEDCA) to register Eskies and collect pedigree information for submission to AKC. Between its inception in 1985 and submission of its records to the AKC in 1993, over 1,750 Eskies were registered with AEDCA. These dogs, along with a few more allowed in an eight-month grace period, form the gene pool for the AKC American Eskimo dog. Incidentally, one more name change had been made: from American Eskimo to American Eskimo dog.

In January 1994, the first American Eskimo dog stepped foot into an AKC ring. Like all new breeds, it made its introduction in the Miscellaneous Class. Most breeds spend a fairly long (several years) term in the Miscellaneous Class while they prove they have adequate support from fanciers, but the Eskie's graduation to regular status was meteoric by AKC standards. In July 1995, the American Eskimo dog was accepted as a regular AKC breed. It is classified in the Non-Sporting group, that eclectic group of dogs that have as their main function that of companion.

One Size Does Not Fit All

One happy result of the Eskie's varied origins is the diversity of sizes present in the breed today. The UKC recognizes two varieties: the standard and the miniature, whereas the AKC recognizes three varieties: standard (over 15 to 19 inches [38.1–45.3 cm]), miniature (over 12 to 15 inches [30.5–38.1 cm]), and toy (9 to12 inches [22.9–30.5 cm]). The bonus of having several sizes from which to choose makes it even easier for prospective owners to find the right dog that suits their lifestyles. At first glance the Eskie appears to be a miniature version of the Samoyed, but closer inspection will reveal that the two are not proportioned the same. The Eskie has smaller bones, and tends to be slightly longer in body than the Samoyed. Nor is the Eskie a larger version of the Pomeranian, again having comparatively smaller bones and a longer body, with not necessarily so profuse a coat.

The Eskie's Future

The American Eskimo dog—a breed both ancient and modern, both ignored and applauded—now faces a new challenge. With its natural flash it is bound to become a favorite at dog shows; but with such popularity comes the danger that the breed will be changed into a caricature of itself. But the Eskie brings with it a group of dedicated breeders who have faced adversity in the past, and who can be trusted to guard the Eskie type and guide it, unadulterated, to a place of prominence in dogdom. And as new owners are attracted to the breed, they will assume a share of the responsibility to protect these spritely little dogs. Perhaps you will be one of these new owners, and will become a part of the new history of the American Eskimo dog.

Selecting Your American Eskimo Dog

So You Want an Eskie?

Maybe it's been in the back of your mind for months. Maybe it just popped in one day. However it got there, the thought just won't go away: you want a dog. A cuddly, playful, beautiful, loyal, obedient, protective, wonderful dog that will make Lassie and Rin-Tin-Tin look like canine underachievers. And you want it now. You want to get in the car and head to Pups-R-Us and bring your bundle of fuzzy love right home. But have you really thought this through?

First, can you make a commitment to this dog for the next 10 to 15 years of your life? When it's no longer the

One of the most outstanding features of American Eskimo dogs is their cheerful disposition.

cutie-pie baby, and ultimately becomes old and frail? Can you make the commitment of time everyday, every *single* day, to feed, groom, exercise, train, and love this dependent being? Dogs make wonderful pets in part because they are almost childlike in their dependence upon their human families, and because they bond so deeply with them. Don't get a dog on a trial basis. If you tire of your dog and think it won't be bothered when you cast it aside, think again. After you have used up its irresistibly cute puppy months, there will be few people lining up to offer it a new home. If the old standby line "Oh, we found him a home in the country" were true, country roads would be impassable with the millions of these former city dogs. The home in the country they found was called the pound, and most of them never left there alive.

Can you make the financial commitment of adding a new family member? The cost of the dog is the least of your worries (and actually, considering the number of years you will have it, a bargain). But food, equipment, boarding, and vet bills can be high. Call several veterinarians' offices in your area and ask the prices for office visits, a series of puppy vaccinations, deworming, yearly checkups, neutering or spaying, emergency clinic visits, and monthly heartworm prevention. There are some companies offering doggy health insurance, but it's not cheap either. But what about making money in dogs? There is no doubt that dogs are a lucrative business—for the pet food industry, pet supply stores, boarding kennels, groomers, veterinarians—in short, everybody you will be paying. But if you plan to make money with your own dogs, the best business decision you can make is to not even get the first one, because it's all in the red after that.

Does everybody in the family want a dog? Now is not the time to be polite and hold your tongue. An unwelcome dog is an unwelcome guest, and neither it nor the resentful family member should have to live together. Don't get a dog just for the children. No matter how sincere the promises to take care of the puppy might be at the time, Mom or Dad will ultimately end up doing most of the work. It is not fair to the pup to use its missed dinner as a lesson to teach Junior the meaning of responsibility.

Think about why you really want a dog. Companionship? Hunting? Protection? Showing? A way to meet people? Think even more about what you *don't* want in a dog. Giant size? Shedding? Aggressiveness? Shyness? Don't choose a breed because your neighbor has one, or it was the star of a recent movie, or it's the current rage, or just because it looks neat. Carefully decide what attributes you want in a dog, and what you don't want; with over 150 recognized breeds in the United States alone, there's very likely a breed out there with your name on it. Maybe it's the American Eskimo dog.

Is This the Breed for You?

Temperament

Most people are initially attracted to a breed because of its looks, and the stunning white Eskie is no exception. But far too often dogs are acquired with the idea that all breeds act the same. They don't. The very reason that different breeds were initially cre-

ated stemmed from differences in behavior, not looks. Dogs were selected for their propensity to trail, point, retrieve, herd, protect, or even cuddle, with physical attributes often secondary to behavioral. Don't get an Eskie and ask it to act like a Doberman or a retriever. It's just not in the genes.

So what is in an Eskie's genes? There are individual differences, but the typical Eskie is an alert, bright, quick-witted dog, wonderfully obedient but sometimes playfully mischievous. The Eskie is loving, demonstrative without being fawning, and is extremely loyal to its family. The Eskie thinks of itself as a family member, and expects to be treated like one. Do not expect an Eskie to be happy if banished to the yard. The Eskie is an excellent watchdog, but does not have the physical attributes to be an intimidating protection dog. Sometimes barking can become excessive. Although not one-person dogs, Eskies

Eskies are active dogs and need room to romp. Here a standard Eskie enjoys the fresh air with a miniature Eskie and miniature pup.

do take a while to warm up to strangers. They *must* be well socialized as youngsters, or this natural wariness can be expressed as shyness and even fear biting. And although Eskies may occasionally be headstrong, in general they are a "soft" breed and tend to be extremely sensitive to harsh words or corrections. In a survey of Eskimo dog owners, barking and digging were listed as the most common problem behaviors, followed by shyness and hyperactivity. Biting, destructive behavior, escaping, and dog fighting were rarely a problem. Some poorly bred Eskies can have nasty temperaments, so you should select your particular Eskie with great care.

Grooming Considerations

Keeping the Eskie's coat gleaming and full and white is not as daunting a task as it might first appear. Its coat texture is such that dirt does not cling, and even mud will fall from the coat as it dries (of course, this may be in your house!). This texture, coupled with a relative lack of oiliness, also tends to be resistant to easy matting, and best of all, the Eskie is virtually free of doggy odor! It is also a good breed for allergic dog owners, as the Eskie sheds minimal dog dander.

Eskies enjoy being groomed, and they should be brushed at least once or twice a week. Males will shed profusely once a year, unspayed females twice a year. During shedding periods they should be groomed more frequently; still, be prepared for your home to be "frosted" with a fine coating of white hair during shedding season.

Health and Longevity

Eskies typically live 12 to 15 years, and do so with minimal health problems. The hereditary health problems so prevalent in most popular breeds have not been reported in American Eskimo dogs. However, as their popularity grows, breeders should not become complacent. Breeders who offer CERF ophthalmological certification or OFA hip certification for their breeding stock are to be commended for their concern and efforts to keep the breed as healthy as it now appears to be.

Finding the Right American Eskimo Dog for You

Now that you have decided that an American Eskimo dog is indeed the dog for you, congratulations—but don't stop now! You'll want to just as carefully locate the right individual for you. And there are still a lot of choices to be made.

Standard, Miniature, or Toy?

After seeing several Eskies, you probably have already formed an opinion about which size most appeals to you. But if undecided, consider that the larger dog will need more room to exercise, take up more room in the car (and bed, if you let it), shed more, and eat more; however, if you want a jogging companion or slightly more intimidating watchdog, the standard should be your choice. The smaller sizes are more vulnerable to attacks from other dogs and injuries from rough children, but may fare better in apartments or as lap dogs. Some of the smaller sizes may be more yappie and active, and also may not be as good with children. True toy Eskies are hard to come by, and will probably be more expensive to purchase. Finally, remember that if you are buying a puppy, breeders can only give you an estimate, not a guarantee, of what size they expect the puppy to be as an adult.

Puppy or Adult?

Although most prospective owners think in terms of getting a puppy, don't dismiss the idea of acquiring an older Eskie. No one can deny that a puppy is cute and fun, but a puppy is much like a baby; you can't ever be too busy to walk, feed, supervise, or clean. If you work or have limited patience, consider an older puppy or adult because it won't require so much intensive care. One advantage of the Eskie's personality is that it is not a "one-person dog", so it can form new bonds fairly easily. On the other hand, an adult may arrive with a host of bad habits; if raised in a kennel, an older dog may have a difficult time adjusting to family life or children.

Most puppies are ideally brought home between 8 and 12 weeks of age, but if you definitely want a show-quality dog you may have to wait until the pups are much older. No matter what the age, if the puppy has been properly socialized your Eskie will soon blend into your family life and love you as though it's always owned you.

Male or Female?

The choice of male versus female is largely one of personal preference, but keep the following pros and cons in mind.

Male Eskies are slightly larger and carry a more profuse coat. They enjoy strutting around and showing off, especially if there is a cute Eskie girl around. Unless neutered, they tend to become preoccupied with sniffing and marking when on walks, and some may also lift their legs in the house. They can also roam in search of female friends, and if they are around one in heat, they are inconsolable. Intact (unneutered) Eskie males do not take well to other intact males, and may fight.

Female Eskies are more delicate in appearance. After each season (or heat), they will shed profusely and lose a good deal of their coats. These seasons occur about twice a year and last for three weeks, during which time you must keep your pet away from amorous neighborhood males who have chosen your house as the place to be. You must also contend with her bloody discharge during her season, either by exiling her from your white carpets (remember the ones you got so her hair wouldn't show up?) or by fitting her with those cute little panties (which she will inevitably be wearing when the person you most want to impress arrives at your home unexpectedly).

Most of the problems associated with either sex can be overcome by neutering. And if the prospects of making more money by breeding an Eskie of one sex as opposed to the other enter into your decision, you should reconsider getting an Eskie at all. You're buying a family member, not livestock; besides, if you depend on the money you could make from breeding Eskies, expect to become very poor!

Pet, Show, or Breeding Quality?

Although at first glance all Eskies pretty much look alike, to the experienced eye there are dramatic differences between individuals. The standard of perfection for the breed does not cover every detail and is open to interpretation in several areas. In addition, some breeders may emphasize flawless movement in their stock, whereas others will sacrifice perfect movement for exquisite facial expression, and still others insist upon a profuse ice white coat. As you see more Eskies from different kennels, these differences will become more apparent to you, and you may begin to form an opinion as to which traits are most important to you. The more subtle differences will probably matter to you only if you wish to acquire a show- or breeding-quality dog. No matter what, the trait that you should never compromise is good temperament. Even a show dog must first and foremost be a pet.

A well-mannered Eskie—whether show-quality, breeding-quality, or just pet-quality—makes a gracious addition to any home.

Pet-quality dogs: Although no dog is perfect, pet-quality dogs have one or more traits that would make winning with them in the show ring difficult. A common reason in males is the failure of one or both testicles to descend into the scrotum. Such dogs can be gorgeous breed representatives, but cannot be shown. However, most veterinarians suggest the retained testicle be removed as it is more cancer-prone, so this is an added expense you must anticipate. Another reason might be any of several small flaws that would never be evident to any but the most ardent Eskie fancier—flaws such as a missing tooth, a long back, or straight shoulders. These, too, make beautiful pets. Somewhat questionable are those with flaws that make them non-Eskie-like (remember, you want an Eskie in part because you like how they look, right?). Such a flaw might be a blue eye, or a very short tail, or oversize. Finally, there are flaws that make pet-quality not even pet-quality: flaws in temperament such as shyness or aggressiveness.

Show-quality dogs: Show-quality dogs should be able to compete in the show ring with a reasonable expectation of finishing a championship. Showing a dog can open an entire new world of exciting wins, crushing losses, eccentric friends, travel to exotic fairgrounds in remote cities, and endless opportunities to spend money. It is inexplicably addicting. You should attend several shows before deciding you want to be a participant. Your search for a show-quality dog will require considerable effort on your part. A show-quality Eskie should be AKC-registered, not just UKC, because the AKC holds many more dog shows. Begin by seeing as many Eskies in real (at dog shows or breeders' homes) and in print (books and magazines) as possible. Ask breeders what they consider to be the good and bad points of their stock. Be forewarned: it will be a rare day when two breeders agree on what is the most perfect Eskie, so in the end it will be up to you alone to make an informed choice based upon your own sense of Eskie esthetics.

Breeding-quality dogs: With few exceptions, breeding-quality dogs come from impeccable backgrounds, and are of even higher show-quality than are show-quality dogs. If you want to breed your dog, start with the very best. Take advantage of the generations of selective breeding behind a quality dog. You may be better off to buy an adult Eskie if breeding-quality dogs is your goal. It is difficult to pick a show-quality puppy at an early age; it is impossible to pick a breeding-quality puppy.

Locating the Perfect American Eskimo Dog

Even if you are not looking for a world beater show dog, you still want to be very careful about where you find your Eskimo dog. Some of the more common sources follow:

Pet shops: Some pet shops flourish on our society's instant gratification lifestyle: go to the mall, get some new shoes, some socks, and an Eskimo dog. A pet shop may be the quickest way to find an Eskie, but because pet shops have many expenses to meet, puppies may be rather costly. Most puppies come from large operations that breed many breeds of dogs. Unfortunately, breeding stock are often poor specimens, and puppies seldom have the advantage of proper socialization. Better pet shops will carefully screen their sources, hire workers to play with and exercise puppies, and provide a health guarantee.

A word of caution about guarantees from any source: no guarantee can reimburse you for your broken heart if your puppy dies. And replacement guarantees that require you to return the original dog aren't worth much when you already love that original dog.

Pet shops are a wonderful source for high-quality dog food, collars, leashes, toys, and many wonderful accessories—but are seldom the optimal source for a new family member.

Newspaper advertisements: If you live in a large city you may find an ad for an Eskimo dog in the paper. Some ads are placed by reputable breeders and could be a good source of a quality pet. But some are not. Look for an ad that says something like:

American Eskimo dogs: Champion sire, obedience titled dam. Reservations taken on show potential and pet puppies available in 3 weeks. Home-raised with children. Health guarantee. $350. Call for information on this versatile breed.

This ad shows that the breeder is concerned with quality by the fact that both parents have some sort of title. The fact that the pups are not yet available shows that the breeder is not trying to simply "move" them at a premature age. By acknowledging that not all pups are show-quality it sounds as though the breeder is willing to make an honest evaluation of the puppies' merits. The pups have been raised in preparation for family life, and this attention to socialization is extremely important. Although you cannot expect a health guarantee to cover everything, the promise of one shows the breeder is confident in the health of the puppies and will stand behind them after the sale. The price is reasonable. Finally, the breeder is interested in informing others about the breed, and would probably be able to tell you if an Eskie really is right for you.

Stay away from ads that look like:

Full-blooded Eskimo spitz puppies! Thoroughbred, registered. Purple ribbon, many champions in pedigree. Shots and wormed. Males $100, females $75.

This ad shows the typical naive backyard breeder at work. It doesn't

No matter where you look for your Eskie, be careful: Eskies are addictive! Luckily their amiable nature enables them to live peacefully with one another.

even have the name of the breed correct, although it is nice that the puppies have all their blood. (Full-blooded is often improperly used to denote purebred, as is the term "thoroughbred," which refers to a breed of horse!) Registered with AKC or UKC? And all UKC-registered Eskimo dogs are now "Purple Ribbon bred," so the term is meaningless. In any pedigree you will find "many champions." A typical pedigree includes over 60 dogs; the law of averages states that several of these would probably be champions, and if these champions are more than two generations back, their genetic effect upon these puppies is negligible. All puppies should be vaccinated and wormed by selling age, so if the breeder considers this a big deal, these pups probably don't have a lot going for them. The price is unre-

alistically low unless many corners have been cut, and there is no reason that one sex should sell for a different amount than the other. They both cost the same to raise.

Friends and co-workers: Evaluate these people the same way as though they had placed an ad. Ask questions such as "Why did you breed the litter?" "How did you choose the sire?" If they answer that they bred the litter because the dam is a good representative of her breed (although not perfect), and they thought she could produce a quality litter if bred correctly, keep listening. If they chose the sire because he was recommended by a breeder as a good complement to their bitch, although a long distance away, put this person on your list of possibles. But if they answer that they bred the litter because "Eskies are fine

Let's play! A Samoyed and an Eskie share a ball.

little moneymakers" or "Fluffy here is Purple Ribbon bred, and Eskies are a rare breed, and although she's never been to a show we were told she's the best one this side of the Ozarks" or that they chose the stud because "He's the biggest Eskimo spitz dog you ever did see, and besides, he lives right down the street," then run away. Do not even look at the puppies lest you get caught up in their undeniable cuteness (*any* Eskie puppy is cute, no matter how poorly bred).

Dog magazines: A quick way to contact several serious breeders is to look in the classified section of one of the monthly dog magazines (such as *Dog World*) available at larger newsstands. The disadvantage is that if the breeder is located a distance from you, you will not be able to evaluate their dogs in the flesh, and you will not be able to choose your own puppy. Also, shipping adds an additional expense and can be stressful for an older puppy.

Dog shows: You can contact the UKC or AKC for the date of a show in your area; these are also listed in *Dog World* magazine. Most shows start at 9 A.M., so unless you know when the Eskies are being judged you must get there early or risk missing them altogether. Tell the Eskie exhibitors of your interest and arrange to talk with several after they have finished in the show ring. Incidentally, don't be swayed by who wins or loses on that one day. It's *your* opinion that matters, not that of one judge.

Why contact a show breeder if all you want is a pet? Because these breeders will have raised your pet as though it were their next Best in Show winner. It will have received the same prenatal care, nutrition, and socialization as every prospective show dog in that litter. And the breeder should be knowledgeable and conscientious enough to have also considered temperament and health when planning the breeding. Most show breeders will demand you stay in touch throughout your dog's life; in fact, you may find yourself part of a very large extended family. Not only does this mean that advice is just a phone call away, but also friendship and help when it's needed. Finally, because in some sense the non-show puppy is a by-product of the litter, these breeders are not out to make a buck from these puppies, and prices are generally quite reasonable.

Breed clubs and rescue organizations: The American Eskimo dog clubs (see Useful Addresses and Literature, page 109) are an excellent source of reputable breeders. In addition, if you are interested in an older dog, consider contacting the breed rescue group, which finds homes for Eskies that have fallen upon hard times.

Animal shelters: Animal shelters may, or may not, be a good source for a pet Eskie. Many dogs are lost or given up through no fault of their own, but many others are brought to the shelter because of health or, more often, behavioral problems. If possible, ascertain why the Eskimo dog was surrendered by its former family, and be forewarned that you may spend more time treating any behavioral problem than is worth the money you save by purchasing from a shelter. On the other hand, there is a certain satisfaction that comes with knowing that you are that dog's savior, and are offering it a life filled with love that it may never have experienced before.

Contacting the Breeder

If you have decided to contact a breeder, you should prepare a list of questions so that you can narrow the field further. Whether you call or write, first tell the breeder how you heard of him or her and exactly what you want. It is not fair to you or the breeder to ask for a show puppy you never intend to show, and it is equally unfair to both of you to get a pet puppy and then try to show it. Many, many hard feelings have arisen because of this seemingly small oversight. If the breeder has a suitable puppy or dog, then expect him or her to ask you something about yourself, your facilities, and your experience with dogs or Eskies in particular. Note: If you really want a show prospect, you will probably have to demonstrate to the breeder that you are serious. You do this by learning as much as possible about American Eskimo dogs and their care before calling, but by also admitting that you don't know it all and are eager to learn.

How often are litters available? If new litters are always in the works, you might worry that the breeder is aiming for profit, not quality. Ask about the parents. Do they have conformation or obedience titles? This is not only important if you want a show/obedience prospect, but again can give you a clue about the care taken with the litter. What kind of temperaments do the parents and the puppies have? If some puppies are being sold as pet-quality, why?

Although you're anxious to see the puppies, now is the time to ask the breeder about the terms of sale. Don't fall in love with a puppy and then have to walk away because an agreement could not be reached. There are several possibilities, the easiest being that you will pay a set amount (usually cash) and receive full ownership. If registration papers cost extra, walk away. Puppy and papers should always be a package deal. If pet-quality, sometimes breeders will insist upon having the puppy neutered before supplying the papers, or they may stipulate that the puppy is to have a "Limited Registration," which means it cannot be shown or bred. If you are making installment payments, the breeder will probably retain the papers or a co-ownership until the last installment. Sometimes a breeder will insist upon co-owning the puppy permanently. If the co-ownership involves future breeding of the puppy and "puppy-back" agreements, you probably should shy away. If the co-ownership is for insurance that the dog will be returned to the breeder in the event you cannot keep it, then such an agreement is probably acceptable. Any such terms should be in writing.

Evaluating the Puppies

Once you have narrowed down your list, if possible arrange to visit the breeder. If you are considering more than one breeder, be honest about it. Always go to view the puppies prepared to leave without one if you don't see exactly what you want. Remember, no good breeder wants you to take a puppy you are not 110 percent crazy about. Don't lead the breeder on if you have decided against a purchase; he or she may have another buyer in line. Finally, don't visit from one breeder to another on the same day, and certainly do not visit the animal shelter beforehand. Puppies are vulnerable to many deadly diseases that you can transmit by way of your hands, clothes, and shoes. How tragic it would be if the breeder's invitation for you to view his or her babies ended up killing them.

Most modern "kennels" are a collection of only a few dogs that are first of all the breeder's pets themselves. However large or small the operation, look for facilities that are clean and safe. Again, these are clues about the care given your prospective puppy.

Does the breeder treat the dogs with love and respect? Even at a young age, mistreatment might have damaged your puppy's temperament. The adults should be clean, groomed, and in apparent good health. They should neither try to attack you nor cower from you. Look to the adults for the dog your puppy will become. If you don't care for their looks or temperaments, say good-bye. The dam will not look her best, so ask to see pictures of her (and the sire) in full bloom. If no such pictures are available, then proceed only with caution.

Finally, the puppies! As you look upon this undulating snowstorm of Eskie-ettes, how will you ever decide? If you want a show puppy, let the breeder decide. In fact, the breeder knows the puppies' personalities better than you will in the short time you can evaluate them, so listen carefully to any suggestions the breeder has even for a pet. But first decide if this is

Hold a puppy by supporting its chest and hind legs. This way, the puppy feels safe from falling and also cannot suddenly wiggle loose.

This mature Eskie seems delighted with his new two-month-old companion—and vice versa!

the litter for you. By eight weeks of age, baby Eskies should look like miniature adults. Of course, they won't have the coat development, or coordination, and their ears may not yet be erect, but they should generally be recognizable as American Eskimo dogs. Dark nose pigmentation, absent at birth, should be present by this age. Normal Eskie puppies are friendly, curious, and attentive. If they are apathetic or sleeping, it could be because they have just eaten, but it could also be because they are sickly. The puppies should be clean, with no missing hair, crusted or reddened skin, or signs of parasites. Eyes, ears, and nose should be free of discharge (although a slight watery discharge from the eyes is not uncommon in Eskies). Examine the eyelids if such a discharge is present to ensure that it is not due to the lids or lashes rolling in on the eye and causing irritation. The teeth should be straight and meet

up evenly, with the top incisors just overlapping the lower incisors. The gums should be pink; pale gums may indicate anemia. The area around the anus should have no hint of irritation or recent diarrhea. Puppies should not be thin or excessively potbellied. By the age of 12 weeks, male puppies should have both testicles descended in the scrotum. If the puppy of your choice is limping, or exhibits any of the above traits, express your concern and ask to either come back next week to see if it has improved, or to have your veterinarian examine it. In fact, any puppy you select should be purchased with the stipulation that it is pending an immediate health check (at your expense) by your veterinarian. The breeder should furnish you with a complete medical history including dates of vaccinations and worming.

You may still find it nearly impossible to decide which bouncing puffball will be yours. Don't worry: no matter which one you choose, it will be the best one. In years to come, you will wonder how you were so lucky to have picked the wonder Eskie of the century—you must realize that your Eskie will be wonderful in part because you are going to make it that way!

Holding the Puppy

These babies are fragile little beings, and you must be extremely careful where you step and how you handle them. If you have children with you, don't allow them to run around or play with the puppies unsupervised. In addition, your entire family should know how to properly handle a puppy. Never pick a puppy up by its legs or head or tail; cradle the puppy with both hands, one under the chest, the other under the hindquarters, and with the side of the pup secure against your chest.

Registering Your New American Eskimo Dog

The breeder should have contacted either the AKC or UKC upon birth of the litter, and received a litter packet containing registration applications for each puppy (green for UKC, blue for AKC). You should not leave with your puppy without the registration application signed by both you and the breeder. This is an extremely valuable document; do not misplace it or forget to send it in! Ask the breeder if there are any requirements concerning the puppy's registered name; most show breeders will want the first name to be their kennel name. You should also have received a pedigree with your puppy; if not, you can buy a copy of its pedigree from the AKC or UKC when you send in the registration papers.

Male or female, puppy or adult, pet or show: congratulations on your new family member!

Choosing between these two healthy youngsters may be impossible!

A Lifetime Shared

You have a lifetime of experiences to share with your new Eskie. The remainder of your little pet's life will be spent under your care and guidance. Both of you will change through the years. Accept that your Eskie will change as it matures: from the cute, eager to please, baby, to the cute, mischievous, often disobedient adolescent, then to the self-reliant adult partner, and finally the proud but frail senior. Be sure that you remember the promise you made to yourself and your future puppy before you made the commitment to share your life: to keep your interest in your dog and care for it everyday of its life with as much love and enthusiasm as you did the first day it arrived home. Your life may change dramatically in the years to come: divorce, new baby, new home— for better or worse, your Eskie will still depend on you and still love you, and you need to remain as loyal to your Eskie as your Eskie will be to you.

Raising Your American Eskimo Dog

One of the most important items to buy is an identification tag. Attach it to the buckle collar.

Welcome Home!

Are you excited? You had better be! If you've done things the right way, you've put a lot of thought into adding this new member of your family; you've decided to share your life for the next 10 to 15 years with an American Eskimo dog! Your life may never be the same.

Once you've chosen your special puppy, you probably can't wait to bring it home. But hold on—it's not fair to either of you to bring a new baby into the house unless you have made all of the necessary preparations beforehand. So channel your excitement, and get the entire family involved, and make sure everything is just perfect for the new addition.

The Christmas puppy: The Christmas puppy is practically an American tradition: such a heartwarming scene is portrayed by the children discovering the baby asleep among the other gifts beneath the tree on Christmas morning. But this is a fantasy scene. The real scene is more often that of a crying, confused baby who may have vented its anxiety on the other gifts and left you some additional "gifts" of its own beneath the tree! Don't bring a new puppy into the hectic chaos of Christmas morning. Not only does this add to what is bound to be a very confusing and intimidating transition for your Eskie, but a puppy should not be expected to compete with all of the toys and games that children may be receiving.

Every pup needs the undivided attention of its new family at this crucial time in its life. Instead, a photograph or videotape of your special Eskie-to-be (perhaps along with some Eskie paraphernalia) will have to suffice until some of the holiday madness has subsided. Meanwhile, the whole family can get involved in preparing for baby.

An Eskie Shopping Spree

If you are a bona fide shopping enthusiast, here's your big chance. Having a new dog will provide you with an excuse to go on a wild shopping spree for all sorts of things your

Begin your shopping spree by buying a round nylon buckle collar for around the house and a nylon, web, or leather leash for taking walks.

Flat-bottomed food and water bowls will not tip over when playful puppies decide to take a dip.

Eskie "just can't do without." A visit to a large pet shop, a dog show vendor aisle, or a glance through one of the pet supply mail-order catalogs will regale you with items you never imagined a dog could need. But even if shopping is not your idea of fun, there are a few essentials you must have. First, your Eskie will need a collar, two collars, in fact. A round nylon buckle collar is best for around the house (flat or leather collars tend to cause matting, staining, and some hair loss). A nylon choke collar is actually safer for walking in public, because a scared puppy can pull backward out of a buckle collar. However, a choke collar is far too dangerous to ever leave on your Eskie unattended. An identification tag should be affixed to the buckle collar. A nylon, web, or leather leash is another necessity. Chain leashes are difficult to handle and tend to smack the puppy in the face, so should be avoided. The retractable leashes are very handy for walking an older puppy, but be very careful not to drop these leashes. When dropped, the handle retracts quickly toward the dog and some puppies think it is chasing them, causing them to run from it in fright!

You will need flat-bottomed food and water bowls. Eskie puppies love to play in water, so be sure the water bowl is not easily tipped. Stainless steel bowls are generally best; some dogs can have an allergic reaction to plastic. Be sure to find out what your puppy is eating and try to feed the same food.

No doubt you have your own bed where you sleep at night. Where will your puppy's bed be? Your Eskie will appreciate having its own bed readily available whenever sleep overtakes it. A cage large enough so that your Eskie can stand and turn around when full grown provides an ideal bed. The cage will also be an invaluable house-training tool, and a means of keeping your puppy out of trouble when you can't always watch. Think of it as you would a baby's crib: a place for peace and protection. And just as with a child, the crib or cage is a place for bedtime and naptime, but not a place of exile or

A cage can be your Eskie's private get-away. Be sure the cage is draft-free and has soft bedding. A hanging water bowl that cannot be spilled completes the bed.

A rawhide chew bone can help keep a teething puppy away from furniture.

can keep an eye on them. Some of the anti-chew preparations may help protect your furniture and walls, but do not rely exclusively upon them. Toys, chewbones, and a keen eye are the best furniture protectors.

Although your young Eskie won't require much grooming, you will still need a soft brush and some nail clippers. The items an adult Eskie needs are described in the grooming section, beginning on page 57. You should also get your first aid kit together, as described in the veterinary section, page 64.

Your Eskie baby will want some toys it can call its own. Rawhide bones are excellent for satisfying the urge to chew. A ball, of course, is a necessity! Many Eskies will take very good care of stuffed animals, and seem to especially enjoy them as toys (make sure the eyes and nose will not come off; also, avoid those stuffed with Styrofoam beads or straw unless you really enjoy vacuuming). Latex squeaky toys are also enjoyable (for them, but not always for their owners!); make sure the squeaker is secure. Homemade toys of plastic milk cartons and stuffed socks are also big favorites. Never give toys that are so

a place to spend entire days. Plastic cages are readily available, economical, and approved for airline shipping. Wire cages allow more ventilation and visibility, and fold for easy storage and transport. Place an easily washed towel or blanket in the cage: Eskies appreciate a soft bed!

You may find an exercise pen (commonly referred to as an "X-Pen") to be a helpful purchase. These are transportable wire folding "playpens" for dogs, typically about 4 × 4 feet (1.2 × 1.2 m). They make a handy indoor enclosure when you can't always be watching. Baby gates are also a big help; puppies do not protest as much when blocked by a baby gate as when blocked by a closed door, plus you

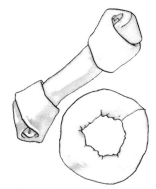

Rawhide chewies come in many shapes. The bone and the ring are two of the more popular.

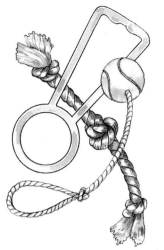

Every youngster needs toys. Good choices for your new Eskie are anything with which to play a good game of tug-of-war.

ing outside. Kitchens and dens are usually ideal. When you must leave your dog for some time, you may wish to place it in a cage, secure room, or outdoor kennel. Garages have the disadvantage of also housing many toxic items; bathrooms have the disadvantage of being so confining and isolated that puppies may become destructive.

If you keep your Eskie outside while you are gone you must provide shelter, preferably a cozy doghouse. The ideal doghouse has a removable top for easy cleaning, and a windbreak so that the door does not lead directly into sleeping quarters. You may wish to place the house within a small absolutely secure kennel for your peace of mind. Some people combine a kennel run with a doggy door leading to an enclosure in a garage, or to a separate room in the house.

small they could be inhaled and lodge in the windpipe. But don't be tempted to use an old shoe; when the pup happens upon your closet full of new shoes, it may think it's arrived at the toy store and start chewing!

Housing Your Eskie

Decide now where you intend to keep your new family member. If you intend to have an exclusively outdoor dog, stop right now and please reconsider your choice of an American Eskimo dog. This breed is not amenable to being kept separated from its family. Although its thick coat enables the Eskie to enjoy cold weather (within reason), hot weather can be intolerable. So plan for your Eskie to spend at least part of its time in the house with the rest of your family.

It is best that the new puppy not have the run of the entire house. Choose an easily Eskie-proofed room where you spend a lot of time, preferably one that is close to a door lead-

Although Eskies love the outdoors, if you're looking for a dog to live exclusively outside, the Eskie is not for you.

27

Eskie-proofing has two goals: protecting your Eskie, and protecting your home. The first step is to do everything you would do to baby-proof your home.

Potential Poisons

Put poisons out of reach—beware of rodent and snail baits, household cleaners, toilet fresheners, leaked antifreeze, drugs, some houseplants, even chocolate (especially baker's chocolate)—all can be deadly. Antifreeze is an especially insidious killer: it has a sweet taste that dogs adore, and a toxic effect that will kill unless treated immediately. Swallowed pennies and nuts and bolts can

Homes are full of items dangerous for puppies. Put them all out of reach, just as you would if you were child-proofing.

If your Eskie will be spending time outdoors, you should provide a doghouse insulated from the elements. This design has an alcove with a small door for protection from the wind and a hinged roof for easy cleaning.

have tragic consequences; they stay in the stomach and gradually dissolve, releasing zinc, which destroys red blood cells. Even nonpoisonous items can be deadly when swallowed. Knives, needles, nails, bones, rocks, rings—all have been found in puppies' stomachs and all have proved fatal at times.

Puppy Obstacles

Get down at puppy level and see what dangers beckon. Look for electrical outlets and cords. Puppies love to chew cords in half, and even lick outlets. These can result in severe burns, loss of the jaw and tongue, and death. Running into a sharp table corner could cause an eye or shoulder injury. Jumping up on an unstable object could cause it to come crashing down, perhaps crushing the

puppy. When cooking, pots should never be where your Eskie could pull them down and be scalded. Do not allow the puppy near the edges of high decks, balconies, or staircases.

Doors can be a hidden danger area. Everyone in your family must be made to understand the danger of slamming a door, which could catch an Eskie and break a leg or tail—or worse. Use doorstops to ensure that the wind does not blow doors suddenly shut, or that the puppy does not go behind the door to play. This can be a danger, because the gap on the hinged side of the door can catch and break a little Eskie leg if the door is closed. Be especially cautious with swinging doors; a puppy may try to push one open, become caught, try to back

28

out, and strangle. Clear glass doors may not be seen, and the puppy could be injured running into them. Finally, doors leading to unfenced outdoor areas should be kept securely shut.

Outdoor Dangers

Now do the same search in your yard. First examine the fence. (If you don't have a fence or enclosure, you've already broken the most essential safety rule.) Make sure it is secure, and that the puppy cannot go over, under, or through it. Do away with sharp edges or wires. Are there bushes with sharp, broken branches at Eskie eye level? Are there poisonous plants? (Some of the more deadly are yew, mistletoe, English holly berries, philodendron, Jerusalem cherry, azaleas, rhododendron, foxglove, water hemlock, milk-

weed, rattlebox, corn cockle, jimsonweed, jessamine, oleander, and castor bean.) If you have a pool, be aware that although dogs are natural swimmers, they cannot pull themselves up a swimming pool wall and can drown.

Finally, you must protect your Eskie against unscrupulous humans, who may find an unchaperoned purebred to be an irresistible source of some imagined easy money. If you leave your Eskie alone in your yard, lock your gate, and take precautions to not make your defenseless friend a target for crime.

Protect Your Furnishings

You've protected your Eskie, now how about your home? Never leave your Eskie puppy in a room in which there is something you would be upset if it were chewed into unrecognizable

Get down at puppy level to properly Eskie-proof your home.

pieces. Leather furniture is the world's biggest rawhide chewy to a puppy. Puppies particularly like to chew items that carry your scent. Shoes, socks, eyeglasses, and clothing must be kept out of the youngster's reach. Remove anything breakable that you value from your Eskie's reach. Remove books and papers. No need for a costly paper shredder when you have a puppy! Move any houseplants that you would like to survive. It's not that Eskie babies are particularly troublesome, but they are puppies—and puppy is just another word for mischief!

If you have carpeting, consider covering it with small washable rugs or a strip of indoor-outdoor carpeting until your puppy is housebroken, at least in the area between the cage and the door. If you use an X-pen, cover the floor beneath it with thick plastic (an old shower curtain works well), and then add towels or washable rugs for traction and absorbancy.

Keep reminding yourself that it's only temporary!

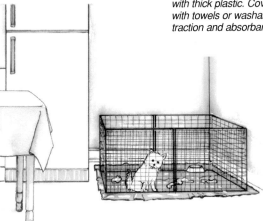

No matter where you place your X-pen, cover the floor beneath it with thick plastic. Cover the plastic with towels or washable rugs for traction and absorbancy.

Bringing Home Baby

It's time! If possible, arrange to take a few days off of work so that you can spend time with your new family member. At the very least, bring the pup home on a weekend so that the first day with you won't be one spent alone. The ride home with you may be the puppy's first time in a car, and its first time away from the security of its home and former family. Be sure to take plenty of towels in case it gets carsick. If possible, bring a family member to hold and comfort the puppy on the ride home. If it is a long ride, bring a cage. Never let a new puppy roam around the car, where it can cause, and have, accidents. Spend some time at the breeder's house while the puppy gets acquainted with you, and listen carefully to the breeder's instructions. Arrange for the puppy not to have eaten before leaving with you; this lessens the possibility of carsickness and helps the puppy learn that you will be its new provider when you get to its new home.

This Eskie puppy explores its new backyard.

Incidentally, be sure to ask the breeder what name your puppy knows. Most breeders call all of their puppies by some generic name, such as "Pup." Just continue to call yours by the same name until you have something better picked out. Your pup will learn a new name quickly at this age, especially if it means food or fun is on the way. Be careful about the name you choose; for example, the ever popular Eskie name "Snowball" unfortunately sounds a lot like "No Ball" and is a confusing choice for a name. Some other bad names: Nomad ("No"), Batman ("Bad"), StayPuff, ("Stay"). Test your chosen name to be sure that it does not sound like a reprimand or command.

When you get home, put the puppy on-lead and carry it to the spot you have decided will be the bathroom. Puppies tend to relieve themselves in areas where they can smell that they have used before. This is why it is so critical to never let the pup have an accident indoors, and if it does, to block its access to that area. Once the puppy relieves itself, let it explore a little and then offer it a small meal. Now is not the time for all the neighbors to come visiting. You want your pup to know who its new family members will be, and more people will only add to the youngster's confusion. Nor is it the time for rough and tumble play, which could scare the puppy. Introductions to other family pets might also be better postponed.

Once the puppy has eaten, it will probably have to relieve itself again, so take it back out to the part of the yard you have designated as the bathroom. Remember to praise enthusiastically when the baby eliminates in the right place. When your Eskie begins to act sleepy, place it in its cage so that it knows this is its special bed. A stuffed toy, hot water bottle, or ticking clock may help alleviate some of the anxiety of being left alone. You may wish to place the cage in your bedroom for this first night so that the puppy may be comforted by your presence. Remember, this is the scariest thing that has ever happened in your puppy's short life; it has been uprooted from the security of a mother, littermates, and loving breeder, so you must be comforting and reassuring on this crucial first night.

Off-limits Training

You should have decided before your puppy came home what parts of your home will be off-limits. Make sure that every family member understands the rules, and that they understand that sneaking the puppy onto off-limit furniture, for example, is not doing the puppy any favor at all. Your puppy will naturally want to explore everywhere you let it, including climbing on furniture. A harsh "No!" and firm push away from the furniture should let it realize that this is neither acceptable nor rewarding behavior. The use of mousetraps on furniture, as advocated by some, is potentially dangerous and not advisable. There are several more humane items (available through pet catalogs) that emit a loud tone when a dog jumps on furniture, but these should not be necessary if you train your young puppy gently and consistently from the beginning.

Housebreaking

All canines have a natural desire to avoid soiling their denning area. As soon as young wolves are able to walk, they will teeter out of their den to relieve themselves away from their bedding. Because you are using a cage for your puppy's den, your Eskie will naturally try to avoid soiling it. But puppies have very weak control over their bowels, so that if you don't take them to their elimination area often,

Eskies never miss a chance to cuddle with their owners.

they may not be able to avoid soiling. Further, if the cage is too large for the puppy, it may simply step away from the area it sleeps in and relieve itself at the other end of the cage. An overly large cage can be divided with a secure barrier until the puppy is larger or housebroken. Even so, just like the wolf cubs, your puppy may step just outside the door of the cage and eliminate there, because to the pup, that fulfills the natural requirement of not going in the den. The puppy has failed to realize that it has just soiled *your* den. And the more the pup soils in a particular spot, the more it is likely to return to that same spot. So, one of the most important keys to successful housebreaking is to never let the first accident occur. Once it has (and more than likely it will), deodorize the area thoroughly, using a non-ammonia-based cleaner, and if possible, place it on the off-limits list, at least temporarily. To avoid accidents, learn to predict when your puppy will have to relieve itself. Immediately after awakening, and soon after heavy drinking or playing, your puppy will urinate. You will probably have to carry a younger baby outside to get it to the bathroom on time. Right after eating, or if nervous, your puppy will have to defecate. Circling, whining, sniffing, and generally acting worried usually signals that defecation is imminent. Even if the puppy starts to relieve itself, quickly but calmly pick the pup up and carry it outside (the surprise of being picked up will usually cause the puppy to stop in midstream, so to speak). You can add a firm "No," but yelling and swatting are neither necessary nor effective. When the puppy does relieve itself in its outside bathroom, remember to heap on the praise and let your Eskie baby know how pleased you are.

If you cannot be with your puppy for an extended period, you may wish to leave it outside so that it will not be forced to have an indoor accident. If this is not possible, you may have to paper train your puppy. Place newspapers on the far side of the room (or X-pen), away from the puppy's bed or water bowl; near a door to the outside is best. Place the puppy on the papers as soon as it starts to relieve itself. A convenient aspect of paper training is that the concept of using the paper will transfer to wherever you put the paper, so if you later take the paper outside it can act as a training tool there.

No matter how wonderful and smart your Eskimo dog is, it probably will not have full control over its bowels until it is around six months of age. Meanwhile, set the stage for a perfect house pet, and chin up! It will get better!

Exercise

As a youngster, your puppy is the best judge of how much exercise is best. Never force a youngster to go beyond its limits; overexercising young dogs has been linked to several developmental skeletal problems. By the time your puppy becomes an adult, you can begin to work up to longer play periods or walking distances. Regular exercise is absolutely essential to good physical and mental health of your dog; plan on at least 20 minutes each day, rain or shine. Walking is an excellent and safe form of exercise; running carries more risks of injury but is undeniably more fun.

If you want your Eskie to enjoy the water, start gradually and get right in there with it. Let your dog play in shallow water until it seems confident. The first time it tries to swim, it will thrash and try to pick its front paws above the water. You can help it learn proper swimming form by elevating its hindquarters and preventing it from lifting its forepaws so high. But even without a "swimming coach," your dog will catch on quickly. Don't push the issue, and with luck you will have an eager aquatic Eskie on your hands.

Eskies and Other Pets

There are certain advantages, and disadvantages, to having more than one dog. Two dogs are twice the fun of one, without being twice the work. Consider adding another pet if you are gone for most of the day. Eskies generally get along well with each other and with other dogs and cats. However, two unneutered males, especially of the same age, are apt to engage in dominance disputes. On the other hand, intact males and females together will provide you with the biyearly problem of keeping Romeo and Juliet separated. Still, Eskies can make close attachments with their housemates, and will enjoy

A child's pool provides respite from hot weather—and a lot of fun!

hours of playing together. In fact, whereas in many ways two dogs are better than one, three dogs are also better than two! With two dogs, a problem can arise when one is left alone while you train or give personal attention to the other. With three, there is always a pair left. Are four dogs better than three? No. Four dogs means one dog too many to catch and hold onto while walking off-lead.

When introducing new dogs, it is best if both are taken to a neutral site so that territoriality does not provoke aggression. Two people walking the dogs beside each other as they would on a regular walk is an ideal way for dogs to accept each other.

Young Eskies are more likely to be hurt by a cat than the other way around. An older Eskie can learn to like cats by introducing them gradually, inside of the house. The dog should be held on a leash initially, and the cat prevented from running, which would elicit a chase response in the dog. If the dog is fed every time the cat

appears, it will come to really appreciate the cat. Many Eskies have become fast friends with "their" pet cats.

Weather Extremes

There are few more breathtaking sights than an Eskie frolicking in the freshly driven snow, a scene of whiteness punctuated only by two gleaming coal eyes, a little black nose, and a happy pink panting tongue. It will come as no surprise that Eskimo dogs like the cold! But even these little snowmen have their limits, and should not be left in extremely cold weather without insulated shelter. Dogs with hair loss problems should wear a coat. Freezing weather brings other hazards. As your Eskie romps in the snow, you must check its feet regularly. Balls of frozen snow will accumulate between the toes and become very uncomfortable; these can be avoided by coating the dog's feet with oil or butter before the walk, or by having the dog wear booties. Walking on streets treated with salt will also be irritating to the paw pads, so be sure to rinse them upon returning home.

Some winter threats can be more deadly. Dogs do not understand that the ice on frozen lakes can break, so you must be vigilant when around thin ice. Be aware of metal items in your yard. Puppies love to lick, and they will lick everything. Tragically, one Eskie puppy lost his tongue (and life) when it froze to a metal object he had licked on a freezing day. Perhaps this story best emphasizes that no matter how diligent you are, puppies have a way of finding unexpected dangers.

Summer has its own list of caveats, the most obvious of which is heat. Many dogs have died of heatstroke because their owners wanted to have them along on a trip to town, and then left them unattended in a poorly ventilated car. Many did not intend to leave them so long, but when they got into the store there was a long line, and in the air-conditioned comfort of the store they lost contact with just how hot it was outside—not to mention, inside a closed car. Heatstroke also occurs as a result of another well-intentioned owner mistake: taking the dog for a walk or run in the summer sun. Dogs do not have sweat glands, and must cool themselves through evaporation from the tongue. This system is not as effective as the human system, and dogs can become overcome by heat when their owners are scarcely affected. Unless you are taking your dog for a swim, leave it at home in the daytime and schedule your outings for early morning or evening. Even if all your dog does is loll in the yard all day, you must provide shade and plenty of cool water to offset heatstroke. Some Eskie owners set up a fan in a safe location, and many provide a child's wading pool filled with water. Incidentally, shaving your Eskie does little, if anything, to improve its cool-

ing capabilities, although removing as much of the undercoat as possible will help. A shaved dog is subject to sunburn and flybites, and besides, looks so very un-Eskie!

With summer also come insect bites and stings. Watch the edges of the ears for fly bites, which can cause a problem. Better yet, use an insect repellent if your dog must stay outside for long periods. If your dog is stung, remove the stinger and watch to make sure there is no allergic reaction. Beware the toad: a large toad secretes a poison that could make a small puppy very ill; the giant marine toad can be deadly.

Summer carries another potentially dangerous event: the Fourth of July. Every year city pounds are filled with lost dogs who fled in terror from noisy fireworks. Many dogs are not claimed, and many are struck in traffic. Secure your dog on this festive occasion, and also during thunderstorms.

Car Manners

The ideal way for your Eskie to travel is in a cage in your car. Still, not everyone can tote around a cage in their little sports car, but there are doggy seatbelts available from pet supply catalogs or pet shops. At any rate, your dog should be taught to sit or lie down quietly when in the car. It should never be allowed to hang its head out the window, where bugs and debris can injure its eyes. And owners who allow their dogs to ride loose in the back of pickups might as well buy a bumper sticker stating "Moron on Board" because that's what they're advertising. Yes, it might look cool for the dog to be precariously balanced on the tailgate, but the ones you don't see are that dog's five short-lived predecessors whose balance or innate sense of fear were not quite so well developed.

Good Fences
Make Good Neighbors

Your Eskie would probably love to go visiting all of your neighbors and help them with their gardening and exercising their cats and all sorts of things that you may think are so very cute and that your neighbor will find so very annoying. Why so many dog owners feel that their dogs are free spirits entitled to rule the neighborhood is inexplicable. Your dog should never, ever be allowed to roam the streets on its own. Not only is it dangerous for the dog, but will make both of you extremely unpopular. Few items can raise the ire of home owners more than dog feces on their lawn, and with good reason. Other people should not be expected to take on your responsibility of cleaning up after your dog. Nor should other people be expected to listen to your dog bark incessantly. It was your decision to bring a dog into the neighborhood, not theirs. As your neighborhood Eskie ambassador, please be an asset to dogdom and to Eskies in particular, and make your dog a good neighbor.

Boarding

Sometimes you have no choice but to leave your Eskie behind when you travel, and may need to board your dog at a kennel or at your veterinarian's. Ask friends for recommendations. The ideal kennel will have climate-controlled accommodations, preferably indoor/outdoor runs. Make an unannounced visit to the kennel and ask to see the facilities. Although you can't expect spotlessness and a perfumy atmosphere, most runs should be clean and the odor should not be overpowering. All dogs should have clean water and at least some dogs should have bedding. Good kennels will require proof of immunizations, and an incoming check for fleas. They will allow you to bring toys and bedding, and will administer medication. Strange dogs should not be allowed to mingle, and the entire kennel area should be fenced.

Your dog may be more comfortable if a pet sitter comes to your home and feeds and exercises your dog regularly. This works best if you have a doggy door.

Don't forget your dog's breeder. He or she may welcome a visit from their former baby, and your Eskie may feel more at home. But be sure that the facilities are safe and escape-proof in case your Eskie decides it wants to go home. Whatever means you choose, always leave emergency numbers and your veterinarian's name.

Lost Dog!

If your little friend escapes or gets lost, you must act quickly in order to ensure its safe return. If your dog has recently escaped, don't wait for it to return. Immediately go to the very worst place you could imagine it

If your pet escapes or gets lost, don't forget to call your local animal control office, police department, and veterinarians. This lost dog was found at the Humane Society.

Few sights are as wonderful to a dog owner as that of a beloved lost pet trotting back home.

going. If you live near a highway, go there, and search backward toward your home. Be certain, however, that your dog does not find you first and follow you to the highway! And if you are driving, be certain that you do not drive recklessly and endanger your own dog's life should it return to you. If you still can't find your Eskie, get pictures of Eskies and go door to door; ask any workers or delivery persons in the area. Call the local animal control, police department, and veterinarians. If your dog is tattooed, contact the tattoo registry. Make up *large* posters with a picture of an Eskimo dog. Take out an ad in the local paper. Mention a reward, but do not specify an amount.

Caution: Never give anyone money before seeing your dog. There are a number of scams involving answering lost dog ads, many asking for money for shipping the dog back to you from a distance or for paying veterinarian

bills—when very often these people have not really found your dog. If your dog is tattooed, you can have the person read the tattoo to you in order to positively identify your pet. Other scammers actually steal your dog for reward money, and wait until you are desperate and will pay a high reward; and then have been known to also burglarize your home when you go to meet their partner to pick up the dog! The moral: Protect your dog in the first place from theft or loss, and be wary when asked for money in return for your dog.

Note: Even license tags cannot always ensure your dog's return, because they must be on the dog to be effective. As your dog runs into the distance after you've bathed your pet and you are left holding an empty collar and tags, you may wish you had a more permanent means of identification. Tattooing is one solution to this problem. Have your Social Security number or your dog's registration number tattooed on the inside of your dog's thigh. You may wish to discuss this option with your veterinarian or local breeders. (See "Useful Addresses and Literature," page 109, for a list of tattoo-based national lost-pet registries.)

The Eskie's World

When you share your world with a dog, you may live in the same place, but you don't experience the same world. Your world is dominated by the visual experience, filled with colors and details.Your dog cannot see the fine details that you can, nor can it appreciate the rich array of colors. Dogs can see colors, but their sense of color is like that of what we commonly refer to as a "color-blind" person. That is, they confuse similar shades of yellow-green, yellow, orange, and red, but can see and discriminate blue, indigo, and violet from all other colors and each other as well as people can.

But before you feel too sorry for them, consider that their sense of smell is thousands of times as acute as yours. It is as though humans are completely blind when it comes to the world of smell, and there is no way one can imagine the vastness of this sensory world that is so very apparent to your pet. The next time you become impatient when your dog wants to sniff something on a walk, consider it the same as when you stop to admire a sunset, much to your Eskie's bewilderment.

Dogs also have a well-developed sense of taste, and have most of the same taste receptors that people do. Research has shown that they prefer meat (big surprise), and although there are many individual differences, the average dog prefers beef, pork, lamb, chicken, and horsemeat, in that order.

Even His Master's Voice may sound different to your dog than to you. Dogs can hear much higher tones than can humans, and so can be irritated by high hums from your TV or from those ultra-sonic flea collars. The Eskie's pricked ears are unencumbered by heavy fur and are ideally suited for detecting and localizing sounds, more so than dogs with other ear configurations.

It is known, of course, that dogs can feel pain. But because a dog may not be able to express that it is in pain, you must be alert to changes in your dog's demeanor. A stiff gait, a reluctance to get up, irritability, dilated pupils, whining, or limping are all indications that your dog is in pain. Some dogs are more stoic than oth-ers, so you must learn to read your individual dog.

Reading Your Eskie

You must become part naturalist in order to fully appreciate this formerly wild species you have invited into your home. Consider the meanings of these displays of dog language:

• What does it mean when your Eskie greets you with a wagging tail and lips pulled back? Most people would think the dog was snarling, but when combined with a happy, submissive greeting, this facial expression is actually known as a "submissive grin."

• What if your dog is lowering its body, wagging its tail, holding its tail down, holding its ears down, urinating, and even rolling over? These are all signs of submissive behavior. Punishing this dog for allegedly snarling would be an injustice.

• What if the dog greeted you with lips pulled back, but with a high, rigidly held tail, hackles raised, perched on its toes, with a stiff-legged gait, a direct stare, forward pricked ears, and perhaps lifting its leg to mark a tree? These are all signs of dominant, threatening behavior. This dog is, indeed, snarling, and you had better leave it alone and get help if it is your dog. Approaching or punishing this dog would likely result in a dog bite.

• What if the dog greeted you with lips pulled back, maybe a little growl, a wagging tail, and its front legs and elbows on the ground and rear in the air? This is the classic "play-bow" position, and is an invitation for a game. Take your friend up on it!

Training Your American Eskimo Dog

That humans and dogs have shared their lives and homes for thousands of years is one of the most amazing relationships in nature. Still, your Eskie is not a little person in a fur suit (as much as it may have you convinced otherwise!), and you cannot expect it to forget its canine roots. You can help your relationship by understanding the dog's nature, and by helping your dog to understand yours.

If you expect your Eskie to be part of the family, then it will need you to show it what is expected of a family member. Because dogs are pack animals, family life is very natural for them. Your family will be your dog's pack now, and just as puppies in a pack look to their mother and the older pack members for leadership, your pup will come to look to you for leadership. Don't let it down. This doesn't mean you have to "show it who's boss"—in fact, just the opposite, because the pup naturally assumes you're the boss unless you convince it otherwise. How would you convince a pup it is the leader? By catering to its every whim, by backing down if it challenges, by never requiring the pup to earn its praise—in short, the same way you would raise a spoiled child! And just as it would be unfair to a child to thrust it into the role of family leader, it is unfair to your Eskie to enable it to be leader.

Many a circus-goer in the early 1900s marveled at the uncanny intelligence and agility of the striking white Eskimo dogs as they regularly performed intricate and sometimes dangerous tricks under the big top. Many of these performers can be found in the pedigrees of modern American Eskimo dogs. So have confidence in your Eskie's ability to learn—it's from the right stuff!

Perhaps the greatest evidence of the dog's intelligence is its ability to learn in spite of many of the commonly employed but totally illogical training methods in use. Just think of what your dog could learn if trained reasonably! Unfortunately, sometimes it seems that everyone who has ever owned a dog is a self-professed expert on dog training. If you follow the tips below, and learn to see the situation from your Eskie's viewpoint, you will be able to evaluate your kindly neighbor's unsolicited advice, and more often than not, politely ignore it! Although no two dogs are alike—and certainly no two American Eskimo dogs—there are some rules that every good Eskie trainer should follow, and some commands every good Eskie should know.

What Every Good Eskie Trainer Should Know

Before trying to train your Eskie, you must train yourself. You must be patient in the face of sessions that seem to make no progress, calm in the presence of an Eskie who may seem determined to do just the opposite of what you desire, jolly in the midst of failure, and clearheaded in the eye of an Eskie storm. You must be consistent, firm, gentle, and realistic.

Name first: The first ingredient in any command is your dog's name. You probably spend a good deal of your day talking, with very few words intended as commands for your dog. So warn your dog that this talk is directed toward it. Say its name first, then follow with a command, and finally help it perform that command.

Then command: Many trainers make the mistake of simultaneously saying the command word *at the same time* that they are placing the dog into position. *This is incorrect.* The command comes immediately *before* the desired action or position. The crux of training is anticipation: the dog comes to anticipate that after hearing a command, it will be induced to perform some action, and it will eventually perform this action without further assistance from you. On the other hand, when the command and action come at the same time, not only does the dog tend to pay more attention to your action of placing it in position, and less attention to the command word, but the command word loses its predictive value for the dog. Again, the sequence is name, then command, and then action. Your Eskie is not hard of hearing. You should not have to shout commands, nor repeat them over and over.

Equipment for training should include a 4 to 6-foot (1.2–1.8 m) nylon, web, or leather lead (never chain), a longer lightweight line of about 20 feet (6 m) and either a buckle collar (for puppies, or for shy, timid, or easily trained dogs) or chain choke collar. The latter has a truly unfortunate name, as it should never be used to choke your Eskie. The proper way to administer a correction with a choke collar is with a gentle snap, then immediate release. The

The correct way to put a chain choke collar on a dog is with the ring and lead coming up around the left side and back of the neck.

lead is attached to the ring that goes through the other ring; this is placed on the dog so that the ring with the lead attached comes up around the left side of the dog's neck. If put on backward, it will not release itself after being tightened (because you will be on the right side of your dog for most training). The choke collar should *never* be left on your Eskie after a training session; there are too many tragic cases where a choke collar really did earn its name after being snagged on a fence, bush, or even a playmate's tooth.

What Every Good Eskie Should Know

Sit

Sitting is a natural position for most Eskies. Your Eskie may even sit on its own when you hold a treat above its eye level. This suggests one easy way to teach your puppy (we've named him Bobby) to sit: Say "Bobby, Sit!"

A well-mannered Eskie is a pleasure in the home and away.

while holding a tidbit at his eye level, then raise the tidbit and move it toward him until it is slightly behind and above his eyes. When he begins to look up and bend his hind legs, praise, then offer the tidbit. Repeat this, requiring his legs to bend more and more until he must be sitting before receiving praise. This is a much more pleasant way for your puppy to learn his first lesson than the traditional push-pull methods of teaching. However, for those Eskies that are not natural sitters, or if you do not wish to use a food reward, you will have to help the dog sit. After commanding "Bobby, Sit!" push the dog backward with your right hand under his chin, and simultaneously push forward, gently, behind his "knees," causing them to buckle and the dog to sit. Praise enthusiastically! You don't want to wrestle your Eskie into a sit. Whichever method you choose, be consistent. Always start by saying "(Dog's name), Sit," followed by

whichever method you have chosen to achieve that sit. And always conclude with lavish praise. You want your Eskie to look forward to these sessions as fun and easy. Eventually

To manually teach "sit," push the dog backwards from the chin while at the same time pushing forward behind the knees.

A young couch potato practices the sit and stay commands.

when your puppy hears "Sit" it will anticipate that you will be helping it to sit—and may just beat you to it!

Stay

After teaching the "sit," the stay command follows. Tell your puppy to "Sit," praise your pet, then say "Stay" in a soothing voice (you do not have to precede the stay command with the dog's name, because you should already have the dog's attention on you). You should be in the same position that you always have been when teaching the sit, either beside or directly in front of the dog. If your Eskie attempts to get up or lie down, gently place it back into position. After only a few seconds, give a release word ("OK!" or "That's All") and praise, praise, praise. After the dog is staying reliably, change your position relative to the dog. If you have been beside it, step out (starting with your right foot) and turn to stand directly in front of it. Again tell the dog to stay, and gently

prevent it from moving. Work up to longer times, and then back away and repeat the process. Eventually you should be able to walk confidently away to longer and longer distances, and for longer and longer times. The point is not to push your dog to the limit, but to let it succeed. To do this you must be very patient, and you must increase your times and distances in very small increments. When the dog does move out of position, return calmly and firmly place it back, repeating "Stay"; then return to your position, then return to the dog while it is still staying so that you can praise.

Hint: Do not stare intently at your Eskie during the stay; it intimidates many dogs and may cause them to move.

Keep in mind that young puppies cannot be expected to sit for more than 30 seconds or so. Work within your Eskie's abilities, correct gently, praise lavishly—and you will have a happy dependable companion.

HOW-TO:
Some Training Tips

• Train in a confined area so your Eskie cannot get out of control. Not only would this be poor training, but also a serious safety risk.
• Train before meals. Your puppy will work better if its stomach is not full, and will be more responsive to treats if you use them as rewards. Never try to train a sleepy, tired, or hot Eskimo dog.
• Keep training sessions short! Dogs have short attention spans and you will notice that after about 15 minutes their performance will begin to suffer. To continue to train a tired or bored dog will result in the training of bad habits, resentment in the dog, and frustration for the trainer. Especially when dealing with an Eskie, boredom can set in quickly with too many repetitions. You will get far better results with short sessions, no longer than 10 to 15 minutes.

Keep your training sessions to 15 minutes because dogs have short attention spans.

Especially when training a young puppy, or when you only have one or two different exercises to practice, quit while you are ahead! Keep your Eskie wanting more, and you will have a happy, willing, obedience partner.
• Begin and end each session with something the dog can do well.
• There is nothing wrong with using food as a reward *as long as you intend to continue using it throughout the dog's life*. If you train a dog using food to tell it that it has done well, and then quit rewarding it with food, the impression to the dog is that it has no longer done well. It may eventually quit performing altogether under these circumstances. If you do use food, precede it with praise; that is, praise, then give a tidbit. Again, the sequence is important. If you give a tidbit and then praise, the dog's impression will be that you are praising it for eating the tidbit—something most Eskies need very little encouragement to do! Also, don't reward with food every time; keep the dog wondering if this will be the time with the tidbit payoff (sort of the slot machine philosophy of dog training). That way, when you can't reward with a tidbit, your Eskie will not be surprised and will continue to perform in the absence of food for comparatively long periods.
• Say what you mean and mean what you say. Your dog takes its commands literally. If you have taught that "Down" means to lie down, then what must the dog think when you yell "Down" to make it jump off

Food is a fine reward for dogs as long as you verbally praise your pet first. Otherwise, your Eskie will think the verbal praise is for eating the reward.

the sofa where it was already lying down? If "Stay" means not to move until given a release word, and you say "Stay here" as you leave the house to go to work, do you really want your dog to sit by the door all day until you get home? One obedience competitor relates the story of how her top obedience dog, trained to jump the high jump at the word "Over," suddenly rolled over on his back when told to do so at a trial. She later discovered that her young daughter had done some training of her own as a surprise for Mom—and taught him to roll over at the command "Over!" (Mom was indeed surprised.)
• Think like a dog. In many ways, dogs are like young children; they act to gratify themselves, and they often do so without thinking ahead to consequences. But unlike young children, dogs cannot understand human language (except for those words you teach them), so you cannot explain to them that their actions of five minutes earlier were bad and must now be

punished. Dogs live in the present; if you punish them, they can only assume it is for their behavior at the time of punishment. So if you discover a mess, drag your dog to it from its nap in the other room, and scold, the impression to the dog will be that either it is being scolded for napping, or that its owner is unpredictable and likely to punish it at random times. This is not the basis for a trusting relationship. Again, remember timing is everything in a correction. If you pull your dog off the sofa and then yell "No," your dog can only conclude that you have yelled "No" to it for getting *off* the sofa. Correct timing would be "No," remove the dog from the sofa, and then praise for now being off the sofa. In this way you have corrected the dog's undesired behavior and helped the dog understand desired behavior.

Say "no" first, then remove your pet from the couch. You don't want your Eskie to think you're reprimanding him for getting off the furniture.

• Corrections should be short-lived. Again, this relates to the dog's inability to relate the present to the past. Owners sometimes try to make this "a correction the dog will remember" by ignoring the dog for the rest of the day. The dog may indeed remember that its beloved owner ignored it, but it will not remember why. Again, the dog can only relate its present behavior to your actions. If you must correct a dog, correct immediately, firmly, without anger, and then be done with it.
• Corrections should never be rough. Such methods as whipping, striking, vigorous shaking by the neck, swinging by the leash, hanging by the collar, or tying items in the mouth have been touted by some trainers:

Do not try them! They are dangerous, counterproductive, and cruel; they have no place in the training of a beloved family member. Eskies, especially, are a sensitive breed and seldom require anything but the mildest of corrections. A direct stare with a harsh "No!" should be all that is required in most cases.
• There is such a thing as over-praising a dog throughout the day. Think of it this way: If you spend the day praising and petting your Eskie just for being there, why should it work for your praise later when it can get it for free? Certainly you should praise, pet, and love your Eskie throughout the day, but in some cases of disobedience and behavior problems such "handouts" must be curtailed. Like the overindulged child whose parents hand him whatever he wants unconditionally, sometimes the overindulged Eskie must learn the value of praise by earning it.
• Be consistent in your training! Sometimes the puppy can be awfully cute when it misbehaves, or sometimes your hands are full, and sometimes you just aren't sure what you want from your Eskie. If you aren't sure what you want, how on earth can you expect a little puppy to know what you want? Once you have a clear picture of what is acceptable and unacceptable behavior, praise the acceptable, and prevent or correct the unacceptable, no matter what. To do otherwise is unfair to the dog. Perhaps the most common inconsistency is letting the pup talk us into something "just this one time." If you let the pup out of its cage because it whines "just this one time," you have taught the pup that although whining may not always result in freedom, you never know, it just might pay off tonight. In other words, *you* have taught the pup to whine.

Come

When both "Sit" and "Stay" are mastered, you are ready to introduce "Come." Your puppy probably already knows how to come; after all, it comes when it sees you with the food bowl, or perhaps with the leash or ball. You may have even used the word "Come" to get its attention then; if so, you have a head start. You want your puppy to respond to "Bobby, Come" with the same enthusiasm as though you were setting down his supper; in other words, "Come" should always be associated with good things.

Caution: Never have your dog come to you and then scold it for something it has done. In the dog's mind it is being scolded for coming, not for any earlier misdeed.

To teach the command "Come," have your Eskie sit, and with the leash attached, command "Stay" and step out to the end of the leash and face your dog. This stay will be a little different for your puppy, as you will drop to your knees, open your arms, and invite him with "Bobby, Come!" in an enthusiastic voice. An unsure pup can be coaxed with a tug on the lead or the sight of a tidbit. Remember to really praise; after all, you have enticed him to break the stay command, and he may be uneasy about that. During the training for come, it is not unusual for there to be some regression in the performance of "Stay" due to confusion; just be gentle, patient, and consistent and this will sort itself out.

The next step is to again place the pup in the sit/stay, walk to the end of the lead, call "Bobby, Come," and quickly back away several steps, coaxing the dog to you. Eventually you can go to a longer line, and run backward as far as your equilibrium will allow. This encourages the pup to come at a brisk pace; in fact, most dogs will regard this as an especially fun game! Of course, in real life, the dog is seldom sitting when you want it to come; so once it understands what you mean by come, allow the pup to walk on-lead, and at irregular intervals call "Bobby, Come," run backward, and when he reaches you be sure to praise. Finally, attach a longer line to the pup, allow him to meander about, and in the midst of his investigations, call, run backward, and praise.

"Come" is the most important command your dog will ever learn. As your dog gets older, you will want to practice it in the presence of distractions, such as other dogs, unfamiliar people, cats, and cars. Always practice on-lead. If it takes a tidbit as a reward to get your Eskie motivated, then this is an instance where you should use an occasional food reward. Coming on command is more than a neat trick; it could save your Eskie's life.

Down

The down command is especially convenient if you need your Eskie to stay in one place for any long periods of time. It is most easily taught with the dog in the sitting position. If you

To manually teach "down," reach under your pet's body and gently ease the front legs forward.

44

are using food rewards, command "Bobby, Down," then show him a tidbit and move it below his nose toward the ground. If he reaches down to get it, give it to him. Repeat, requiring him to reach farther down until he has to lower his elbows to the ground. You can help him out here by reaching under him and easing his front legs out in front of him. If you do not wish to use food rewards, again start with the dog sitting, command "Bobby, Down," then reach over his shoulders with your left arm to grasp his left foreleg just below the elbow, and grasp his right foreleg in the same place with your right hand, and ease him to the ground. Some submissive dogs may become frightened using this latter method, and some dominant type dogs will fight being forced to the ground. However, if praise is heaped upon them, both types will eventually accept this new part of the obedience game. Practice the down/stay just as you did the sit/stay. In fact, your dog now has quite a repertoire of behaviors that you can combine in different ways to combat boredom. The only thing left for any well-behaved Eskie is the ability to walk politely on-lead.

Heel

Whenever an Eskie and its owner walk down the street, they are bound to attract attention. Hopefully the picture created will not be one of a lunging, choking, white whirlwind dragging you behind, but of a happy, confident, and responsive companion walking alongside of you as a team. A well-trained Eskie can walk with its owner through crowded sidewalks or dog show aisles, neither pulling, lagging, nor getting underfoot, with the dexterity and timing of a dance partner. But such precision is not immediate, and you should not ask such perfection of your beginning Eskie. In fact, in a very

young Eskie, the first step is to introduce your pet to the leash. If you have followed this training sequence, it should already be acquainted with the leash at least by the time your dog has learned "Come." Still, walking alongside of you on-lead is a new experience for a young baby, and many will freeze in their tracks once they discover their freedom is being violated. In this case, do not simply drag the pup along, but coax it with praise, and if need be, food, until it's walking somewhere—anywhere. Take turns letting the puppy lead and you lead. When you lead, praise and reward. In this way the pup comes to realize that following you while walking on-lead pays off.

Once your Eskimo dog walks confidently on-lead, it is time to ask for more. With the leash on, have your Eskie sit in the heel position; that is, on your left side with its neck next to and parallel with your leg. Say "Bobby, Heel" and step off with your left foot

An Eskie in proper heeling position moves in step alongside but out of the way of the handler.

first. During your first few practice sessions, keep him on a short lead, holding him in the heel position, and of course praising him. When you stop, have him sit. Although some trainers advocate letting the dog lunge to the end of the lead and then snapping it back, such an approach is unfair if you haven't shown the dog what is expected of it at first, and such methods often make for unhappy heelers or even laggers. Instead, after a few sessions of showing the dog the heel position, give it a little more loose lead; if it stays in the heel position, praise; more likely it will not, in which case pull your pet back to position with a quick snap, then release, of the lead. For adult dogs who still seem totally oblivious to the fact that you are trying to teach them something, there is a simple solution. Let your pet forge ahead; as soon as the dog does so, make an unexpected about-turn or right turn; the dog will soon realize that you can be unpredictable and that it had best keep an eye on you. After each correction, be sure to praise as you help your dog into the heel position.

Warning: Too many such corrections may result in a dog that lags behind you, as it realizes the best place to keep you under surveillance is from the rear. And lagging dogs are extremely difficult to speed up, so much so that they are known as the obedience competitor's curse.

A common mistake that new trainers make is to walk too slowly; a slow walk gives dogs time to sniff, to look all around, and in general become distracted; a brisk pace will focus the dog's attention upon you and generally aid training. As you progress, you will want to add some right, left, and about turns, and walk at all different speeds. Then practice in different areas (still always on-lead) and around different distractions. Vary your routine to combat boredom, and

keep training sessions short. Adult dogs should be taught that heeling is not the time to relieve themselves.

Higher Education

You may find that you and your Eskimo dog have enjoyed these sessions; in fact, you may be thinking of your Eskie as "gifted." Perhaps you would like to learn more, or be able to practice with other dogs around, or discuss problems with people who have similar interests. Most cities have obedience clubs that conduct classes. Many include puppy kindergarten classes so that young dogs can be properly socialized. Some clubs will advertise in the newspaper or phone book, but you can also contact the American Kennel Club or your local Humane Society for the name of someone to contact in the club nearest you. You might also contact one of the American Eskimo dog breed clubs and ask for names of Eskie obedience enthusiasts in your area. Attend a local obedience trial (contact the AKC for date and location) and ask local owners of happy working dogs (especially Eskies!) where they train. Be aware that not all trainers may understand the Eskimo psyche, and not all classes may be right for you and your Eskimo dog.

You may wish to enter an obedience trial yourself eventually, in which case the advice of fellow competitors will be invaluable. Obedience competitors love their sport; they love to welcome newcomers, and they love to see them succeed; most of all they love their dogs and understand how you love yours. Eskies are adept obedience pupils, and your Eskie and you could very well become an award-winning team.

Behavior Problems

Asking Eskie owners about their dogs' behavior problems is like asking doting parents about their child prodigies' behavior problems—you don't get a lot of answers! But though they may look like little darlings in snowsuits, under that innocent disguise even Eskies are still dogs and share the behavioral problems to which all dogs are prone.

Carsickness

Nothing can spoil the vision of you and your gleaming white puppy sharing a tranquil drive in the country like the reality of that puppy being covered with its own drool, or worse! Carsickness is a common ailment of puppies; most outgrow it, but some need car training in order to overcome it. Car rides should be made extremely short, with the object being to complete the ride before the dog gets sick. This may mean going only to the end of the driveway, and then working up to the end of the block. Driving to a place where the dog can get out and enjoy itself before returning home also seems to help the dog look forward to car rides and overcome carsickness. Motion sickness medication may be prescribed by your veterinarian to help in stubborn cases.

Jumping Up

Although it may seem so cute when your baby Eskie puts its paws on your leg and looks adoringly into your eyes, your guests will probably not appreciate your full grown Eskie jumping on their new clothes or on their children. Eskies may be smart, but even Eskies cannot discriminate whether you are wearing new clothes or old, nor whether their own paws are muddy or clean. The simplest solution is to avoid the problem in puppies by crouching down so that your face is at a level that does not require the dog to jump up. When you are standing, a quick step backward so that the pup's feet meet only air is often sufficient discouragement. Older dogs can be told to sit and stay while greeting the owner or guests, who may or may not wish to crouch down to the dog's level. A highly excitable dog may be distracted by a thrown ball or by being stepped into when it begins to jump up. All too often dogs are banished to the yard permanently because they insist on jumping on people; unfortunately, the isolated dog will be so thrilled when it is visited by its owner that the jumping up behavior will only get worse. Remember, your Eskie is glad to see you; don't punish it for its greeting but guide it to a civilized greeting.

Barking

Barking is a natural and useful trait of dogs, and Eskies are natural watchdogs. But the surest way to make your neighbors dislike your Eskie is to let it bark excessively, and besides, a watchdog that barks all the time is like the watchdog who cried "wolf!" When the real intruder comes, nobody will pay any attention. Allow your Eskie to bark momentarily at strangers, and then call it to you and praise it for quiet behavior. The best watchdogs are those that sound the alarm, seek out the owner, and then await the owner's command.

Puppies who are isolated will often bark as a means of getting attention and alleviating loneliness. Even if the attention gained includes punishment, the pup will continue to bark in order to obtain the temporary presence of the owner. The simplest solution is to move the dog's bed to a less isolated location. If this is not possible, the pup's quiet behavior must be rewarded by the owner's presence, working up to gradually longer and longer periods. The distraction of a special chew toy, given only at bedtime, may help alleviate barking. The pup who must spend the day in the yard alone is a greater challenge. Again, the simplest solution is to change the situation, perhaps by adding another animal to the yard—a good excuse to get two Eskies!

"Hole? What hole?" Eskies are notorious diggers.

Digging and Chewing

One of the best things about owning an American Eskimo dog is the joyous greeting you are bound to receive upon your return home. But this heartwarming reunion can be greatly cooled by the sight of your home in shambles. Home destruction accounts for more dogs being exiled to the yard, or worse, the pound, than any other behavioral problem. But given proper training, your Eskie and your furniture can learn to coexist peacefully.

Puppies dig and chew. Your job is to see to it that they don't dig where you don't want them to and they don't chew what you don't want them to. The provision of a sandbox for digging and a variety of chew toys will save you many dollars in sod, shoes, and furniture—as long as you still monitor the pup so that it never has a chance to dig or chew the wrong things. Adult dogs may dig or destroy items through frustration or boredom. The best way to deal with these dogs is to provide both physical interaction (such as chasing a ball) and mental interaction (such as practicing a few simple obedience commands) on a daily basis. But be forewarned: Eskies are notorious diggers! You may simply have to fence off your prize-winning garden, or not allow your Eskie to play unsupervised.

One of the most common causes of destructive behavior is also one of the most misunderstood: separation anxiety. Some angelic Eskies turn into demolition dogs when left alone. The owners attribute this Jekyll and Hyde behavior to the dog "spiting" them for leaving, or think that their dog only misbehaves then because it knows it would be caught otherwise. But an observant owner will notice some things that are different about the dog that destroys only when left alone. For one, the dog often appears to be in a highly agitated state when the owner returns. For another, the sites of destruction are often around doors, windows, or fences, suggestive of an attempt to escape. Such dogs are reacting to the anxiety of being left alone; recall that for a social animal this is a highly stressful situation. But the average owner, upon returning home to such ruin, punishes the dog. This in no way alleviates the anxiety of being left alone; it does, however, eventually create anxiety associated with the owner's return home, and this tends to escalate the destructive behavior. Dogs seem to understand "when the house is in shreds and my owner appears I get punished" but not to understand "when I chew the house it gets messed up and I will get punished when my owner appears." If they did, punishment would remedy the problem. It does not. Instead, owners must realize that they are dealing with a fear response: the fear of being alone. The foolhardiness of punishing a dog for being afraid should be obvious. Instead the dog must be conditioned to overcome its

48

fear of separation. This is done by separating the dog for very short periods of time and gradually working to longer periods, taking care to never allow the dog to become anxious during any session. This is complicated when the owner *must* leave the dog for long periods during the conditioning program. In these cases, the part of the house or yard in which the dog is left for long periods should be different from the part in which the conditioning sessions take place; the latter location should be the location in which the owner wishes to leave the dog after conditioning is completed. In either case, when the owner returns home, no matter what the condition of the home, greet the dog calmly or even ignore it for a few minutes, to emphasize the point that being left was really no big deal. Then have the dog perform a simple trick or obedience exercise so that you have an excuse to praise it. It takes a lot of patience—and often a whole lot of self-control—but your Eskie can learn to accept being home alone.

House soiling

When a dog soils the house, several questions must be asked. The first is obvious: was the dog ever really completely housebroken? If the answer is no, you must begin housebreaking anew (see Housebreaking, page 31). Sometimes a housebroken dog will be forced to soil the house because of a bout of diarrhea, and afterward will continue to soil in the same area. If this happens, restrict that area from the dog, and revert to basic housebreaking lessons once again. Submissive dogs may urinate upon greeting you; punishment only makes this "submissive urination" worse. Keep greetings calm, don't bend over or otherwise dominate the dog, and usually this can be outgrown. Some dogs defecate or urinate due to the stress of separation anxiety; you must treat the anxiety (see Digging and Chewing, page 48) to cure the symptom. Older dogs may simply not have the bladder control that they had as youngsters; paper training or a doggy door is the best solution for them. Older spayed females may "dribble"; ask your veterinarian about estrogen supplementation, which may help. And even younger dogs may have lost control due to an infection; several small urine spots are a sign that a trip to the vet is needed. Male dogs may "lift their leg" inside of the house as a means of marking it as theirs. Castration will solve this problem; otherwise diligent deodorizing and the use of some dog-deterring odorants (available at pet stores) may help.

Escaping and Roaming

Keeping your Eskie in an enclosed area not only makes it a more welcome neighbor, but also an Eskie with a longer life expectancy. But sometimes the Eskie doesn't see it that way. It is more enticing to visit the local schoolyard, go calling on a lady dog, or hang out with its stray buddies. Find out the reason for your dog's travels. If it is for human or canine interaction, arrange to spend more time with your Eskie and for your Eskie to have supervised play with a canine friend. One Eskie owner relates that her dog becomes upset if he cannot visit with the children at the school bus stop—so the owner walks him there on a lead every morning! The male who roams looking for females can be effectively cured by castration. Although it is tempting to punish the roamer when caught, in the long run this is counterproductive as dogs may learn that coming to you results in punishment.

The most effective cure is prevention, by making a yard that is escape-proof from the very beginning. Many

Don't let your Eskie run free. At home, keep your pet in the house or fenced yard. On the road, always use a leash.

Fearfulness

A gregarious breed by nature, nonetheless, the American Eskimo dog is somewhat conservative with strangers, and there may be times when your Eskie may act shy or fearful. Your Eskie should never be pushed into situations that might overwhelm it. A program of gradual desensitization, with the dog exposed to the frightening person or thing and then rewarded for calm behavior, is time-consuming but the best way to alleviate the fear. Never force a dog who is afraid of strangers to be petted by somebody it doesn't know; it in no way helps the dog overcome its fear and is a good way for the stranger to get bitten. Strangers should be asked to ignore shy dogs, even when approached by the dog. Dogs seem to fear the attention of a stranger more than they fear the strangers themselves. It is always useful if your Eskie knows a few simple commands; performing these exercises correctly gives you a reason to praise the dog and also increases the dog's sense of security because it knows what is expected of it. In any attempt to overcome fear, the most important rules are also the most tempting to break: never hurry, and never push the dog to the point that it is afraid.

Aggression

No matter what size Eskie you own, its teeth are large enough to do considerable damage. The best cure for aggression is prevention, and the best prevention is to carefully select your Eskie from a responsible breeder. Poorly bred Eskies have developed a reputation as an untrustworthy breed, but knowledgeable breeders have worked hard to develop trustworthy companions. Truly aggressive well-bred Eskies are very unusual, and in most cases the cause can be traced to one of several family situations.

dogs are actually inadvertently taught to escape by their owners. First enclosures are often adequate for young pups, but as the puppy grows, the enclosure can no longer contain it. For example, a 2-foot (0.6 m) high fence can hold the baby Eskie but the adult Eskie finds it can jump right over. At this point, many owners make some sort of minimal repair, such as increasing the fence height by a few inches. With a little more effort, the Eskie clears this height. Another few inches are added, until, a few inches at a time, the frustrated owner finally realizes that he has coached his Eskie to Olympic jumping abilities. If you wanted your Eskie to learn to jump high fences, wouldn't you build up to it a little at a time? Then why use the same tactic to teach your dog *not* to scale high fences? If you want your dog to stay in the yard, make the yard Eskie-proof from the very beginning.

Eskies love to romp—in snow, in grass, in anything. Owners need to remain alert, however, because a romping Eskie can quickly become a roaming Eskie.

Some Eskies may bite out of fear, perhaps because the owner is pulling them by the collar to a feared location. The solution is to find out what the dog is afraid of and use the gradual desensitization method outlined above. Be aware that unlike in humans, where direct eye contact is seen as a sign of sincerity, staring a dog directly in the eye is interpreted by the dog as a threat. It can cause a fearful dog to bite out of what it perceives as self-defense.

Eskies have an innate tendency to defend their territory; however, they should not threaten guests you have welcomed into your home. Teach your Eskie to look forward to guests by rewarding proper behavior, such as sitting and staying, in the guests' presence.

Some dogs will bite out of resentment, such as the dog that is hustled out of the house when company arrives, or in the presence of a new baby. Again, the solution is to teach your Eskie to respond to simple commands such as sit and stay, and use them to help the dog be well mannered in the presence of guests or the baby. In drastic cases, attention can be withheld from the dog except in the presence of guests or the baby, so that the dog associates being with them as something that brings itself attention and rewards. Of course, it should hardly be mentioned that no baby or child should be allowed to play roughly with or tease your Eskie. The smaller varieties of Eskimo dogs are not as well suited for young children; because the mini and toy Eskies can be more easily hurt by rough play, they may become aggressive out of self-defense.

Any dog that is socially isolated is more apt to become aggressive; and, once aggressive, more apt to be kept isolated. Perhaps the most common cause of aggression is the practice of some pet owners to tie out their dogs. A dog that is tied out with a view of the family having a good time becomes frustrated at not being able to join in; this frustration eventually often vents itself as aggression. You should reconsider getting an Eskie if you do not intend to make it a real part of your family.

Some cases of aggression occur when a dominant dog believes its owner to be its subordinate; when the owner tells it to do something, it refuses, and if pushed, may bite the owner. Such behavior is rare in Eskies, but can happen if an owner has not established a proper leadership role. Always allowing the dog to have its way, allowing it to lead on walks, feeding it on demand, petting it for no reason—all of these actions can lead the dominant-type dog to conclude that it is the leader of the pack. Owners must stop these behaviors, and establish themselves as leader; again, the simplest way is by the use of obedience exercises.

Aggression toward other dogs or animals is also uncommon in Eskimo dogs. It most often arises through territorial (in the case of strange dogs) or dominance (in the case of familiar dogs) disputes. When you walk your Eskimo dog down the street and it urinates on the trees lining the way, your pet is marking its territory. When the neighbor's dog does the same thing, both dogs mistakenly believe that street to be their territory—and when they meet, they may fight for it. Dogs that are aggressive toward other dogs can be held in check somewhat simply by preventing them from marking. More problematic is the case where two dogs that live together do not get along. Dogs may be vying for dominance, and fights will occur until one dog emerges as the clear victor. But even in cases where one dog is dominant, fights may erupt when both are competing for the owner's attention. The dominant dog expects to get that attention before the subordinate, but being a fair-minded owner, you may tend to give attention equally, or to even favor the "underdog." This can be interpreted by the dominant dog as an uprising by the subordinate dog, who is then attacked. This is one case where playing favorites (to the dominant dog) will actually be a favor to the subordinate dog in the long run!

When All Else Fails

Chances are you and your Eskie will live together blissfully with never a major behavioral problem. But if a problem does arise that you are unable to solve, consult your veterinarian. Some problems have physiological bases that can be treated. Also, your veterinarian may refer you to a specialist in canine behavior problems.

Feeding Your American Eskimo Dog

"You are what you eat" is just as true for dogs as it is for people. Because your Eskie can't go shopping for its dinner, it "will be what you feed it," so you have total responsibility for feeding your dog a high-quality balanced diet that will enable it to live a long and active life. Dog food claims can be conflicting and confusing, but there are some guidelines that you can use when selecting a proper diet for your Eskie.

First, the Association of American Feed Control Officials (AAFCO) has recommended minimal nutrient levels for dogs based upon controlled feeding studies. Unless you are a nutritionist, the chances of you cooking up a homemade diet that meets these exacting standards is remote. So the first rule is to select a food that states on the label that it meets the requirements set by the AAFCO. You should also realize that when you add table scraps and other enticements, you are disrupting the balance of the diet.

Second, feed a high-quality food from a name-brand company. It is always surprising that owners who may have paid a hefty price for a pure-bred puppy will feed an inferior food in order to save a few cents a day, and at the same time think nothing of spending the price of a month's supply of dog food on a single gourmet meal for themselves! Higher price does not necessarily mean higher quality, but very low price may indicate that inferior products would have to be used to enable the company to make a profit.

Third, find a food that your Eskie enjoys. Mealtime is a highlight of a dog's day; although a dog will eventually eat even the most unsavory of dog foods if given no choice, it hardly seems fair to deprive your family member of one of life's simple, and for a dog, most important, pleasures.

A Can, a Bag, or a Pouch?

There are a number of high-quality palatable foods on the market from which to choose, but one of your first choices will be which form of food to feed. Dog foods come in several varieties, each with advantages and disadvantages. Dry food is the most popular and economical, but most dogs find it the least palatable. It is also probably the healthiest, both in nutrient level and for dental hygiene. It is doubly important that dogs fed dry food have water available at all times. Canned foods are also popular, but most people feed them as an additive to dry foods to increase palatability. Their high moisture content helps to make them tasty, but it also makes them comparatively expensive, because you are in essence buying water. A steady diet of canned food would not provide the chewing necessary to maintain dental health. Semi-moist foods are popular with some owners, but these too cannot provide proper chewing and also have the disadvantage of being fairly expensive and loaded with preservatives (mostly sugar-based). But many dogs enjoy them so they can be a reasonable

Dog food comes in three major forms—dry, canned, and packaged.

choice for use in conjunction with a high-quality dry food. They are also very convenient when traveling. Dog biscuits provide excellent chewing action, and some of the better varieties provide complete nutrition, but they can be expensive and most people use them for snacks.

Read the Fine Print

When comparing food labels, keep in mind that differences in moisture content makes it virtually impossible to make comparisons between the guaranteed analyses in different forms of food. The components that vary most from one brand of food to another are protein and fat percentages.

Protein: Many high-quality foods boast of being high in protein, and with good reason. Protein provides the necessary building blocks for growth and maintenance of bones and mus-

cle, and in the production of infection fighting antibodies. The best sources of protein are meat-based, but soybeans are also a popular source. Puppies and adolescents need particularly high protein levels in their diets, which is one reason they are best fed a food formulated for their life stage. Older dogs, especially those with kidney problems, should be fed much lower levels of very high-quality protein.

Fat: Fat is the calorie-rich component of foods, and most dogs prefer the taste of foods with higher fat content. Fat is necessary to good health, aiding in the transport of important vitamins and providing energy. Dogs deficient in fat often have sparse, dry coats. A higher fat content is usually found in puppy foods, whereas obese dogs or dogs with heart problems would do well to be fed a lower fat food.

Some fat in food is necessary for good health. Dogs deficient in fat have sparse, dry coats. This Eskie eats the right amount.

Choose a food that has a protein and fat content best suited for your dog's life stage, adjusting for any weight or health problems (there are a number of special diets available from your veterinarian especially designed for specific health problems). Also examine the list of ingredients: a good rule of thumb is that three or four of the first six ingredients should be animal derived. These tend to be more palatable and more highly digestible than plant-based ingredients; more highly digestible foods mean less stool volume and less gas problems.

Finally, let your Eskie help you choose. Find a food that your dog likes, one that creates a small volume of firm stool and results in good weight with a full coat. Be aware of the signs of possible food allergies (loss of hair, scratching, inflamed ears). You may have to do a little experimenting to find just the right food, but a word of warning: One of the great mysteries of life is why a species, such as the dog, that is renown for its lead stomach and preference to eat out of garbage cans, can at the same time develop violently upset stomachs simply from changing from one high-quality dog food to another. But it happens. So when changing foods you should do so gradually, mixing in progressively more and more of the new food each day for several days. Also, dogs will often seem to prefer a new food when first offered, but this may simply be due to its novelty. Only after you buy a six-month supply of this alleged canine ambrosia will you discover it was just a passing fancy.

How Much, How Often?

Very young puppies should be fed three or four times a day, on a regular schedule. Feed them as much as they care to eat in about 15 minutes. From the age of three to six months, pups

The proper diet produces an Eskie that is healthy, happy, and gorgeous.

should be fed three times daily, and after that, twice daily. Adult dogs can be fed once a day, but it is actually preferable to feed smaller meals twice a day. A geriatric dog will especially benefit from several small meals rather than one large one. Some people let the dog decide when to eat by leaving dry food available at all times. If you choose to let the dog "self-feed," monitor its weight to be sure it is not overindulging.

Proper Eskie weight is in the range of 5 to 7 pounds for toys, 10 to 20 pounds for minis, 25 to 35 pounds for standards. You should be able to just feel the ribs slightly when you run your hands along the ribcage; in addition, when wet, there should be an indication of a waistline, both when viewed from above and from the side. If your Eskie is fat, do not allow it to continue overeating. Try a less fattening food or feed less of your current food; make sure family members aren't sneaking it tidbits. If your Eskie remains overweight, seek your veterinarian's advice. Obese Eskies miss out on a lot of fun in life, and are prone to joint injuries and a shortened life span.

Finicky eaters are another special challenge. Many picky eaters are created when their owners begin to spice up their food with especially tasty treats. The dog then refuses to eat unless the preferred treat is offered, and finally learns that if they refuse to eat even that proffered treat, another even tastier enticement will be offered. Give your Eskie a good, tasty meal, but don't succumb to Eskie blackmail or you may be a slave to your dog's gastronomical whims for years to come. Luckily, most Eskies are far too gluttonous to exhibit the self-control necessary for such a ruse.

Coprophagia: Even Good Dogs Eat Bad Things

Stool eating: Few dogs are more difficult to comprehend than those that stick up their noses at gourmet dog food and then sneak a feast from the cat's litter box at the first opportunity. But the sad truth is that all dogs, Eskies included, consider cat, rabbit, and various livestock feces a special delicacy. Many explanations have been advanced (and discarded) for why what is so vile to us is so enticing to them, but whatever the reason, it is still scant consolation the next time

Never Feed
• Chicken, pork, lamb, nor fish bones. These can be swallowed and their sharp ends can pierce the stomach or intestinal walls.
• Any bone that could be swallowed whole. This could cause choking or intestinal blockage.
• Supplemental minerals of any type unless specifically prescribed by a veterinarian.
• Chocolate. Contains theobromine, which is poisonous to dogs.
• Alcohol. Small dogs can drink fatal amounts quickly. Drunk and alcoholic dogs are not cute.

your Eskie tries to kiss your face after indulging! But don't be ashamed if your Eskie woofs down a forbidden morsel; it is very common. Just do your best to keep the litter box out of reach and realize that dogs aren't quite as human as you would like to believe!

Less tolerable is the dog that eats its own feces. A number of theories have been advanced to explain this most repulsive of eating habits: boredom, nutritional deficiency, filth; but none is adequate to explain all instances. Food additives are available to make the stool less savory, but the best cure is prevention by fastidious poop-scooping. Many dogs experiment with feces eating as pups, but most will grow out of it.

Grooming Your American Eskimo Dog

That white powder-puff coat is no doubt one of the Eskie's most undeniable charms, and probably one of the main attributes that drew you to the breed. The upkeep of such a crowning glory may at first seem intimidating, but a short grooming session once or twice a week will usually suffice to keep both you and your Eskie proud. Of course you can rely upon a professional dog groomer, but in truth you will ultimately find it easier and more relaxing to do it yourself. You will save money, and your dog will appreciate not having to spend the day with strangers. Besides, the end result will be better; the upkeep of an Eskimo dog requires a little grooming often, rather than a lot of grooming seldom.

You may wish to use a grooming table, but it is equally effective to have the dog lie on a towel while being brushed. Many dogs and owners look forward to such grooming sessions as a relaxing time of bonding. Of course, if your Eskie is screaming and kicking and you're grabbing and pulling you will probably achieve relatively little relaxation or bonding from the experience. Start right, by grooming your puppy before it's had time to develop any tangles, so brushing feels even better than petting to the pup. Make a routine of spending just a few minutes every day devoted to this special kind of petting. Keep each session short, fun, and rewarding. In the puppy, you need not follow the full grooming routine; remember, although you certainly want to prevent the formation of any tangles, your most important long-term goal now is training the pup to be cooperative.

You may be faced with some coat disasters on occasion. Chewing gum can be eased out by first applying ice; pine tar can be loosened with hair spray; other tar can be worked out with vegetable oil followed by dishwashing detergent; tight mats and burrs can be helped by soaking for an hour in tangle remover or vegetable oil; and skunk odor may be helped by tomato juice. Use a soft toothbrush to work on stains. Avoid eye stains by diligent use of an eye stain preventative such as Diamond Eye drops. Use mineral oil to loosen debris in the ear.

Coat and Nail Trimming

You can tidy up the feet by carefully trimming the shaggy hairs so that the foot appears small, neat, and compact. Brush the hair on the rear of the hock upward and trim the ragged edges parallel to the bone. Even if you are not trying to create a show dog look, trimmed feet track in less mud. The American Eskimo dog is an exception to the general rule that show dogs must have their whiskers trimmed. It is a credit to the fanciers of this breed that they demand these important sensory organs remain intact on their dogs whether at home or in the ring.

Trimming and fluffing is optional for everyday life, but nail trimming is not. Begin by handling the feet and nails daily, and then "tipping" the ends of

A soothing voice and gentle touch are important tools for cutting nails.

Hold your dog's feet behind it, so that you are looking at the bottoms of the toenails. Then cut the tip to the core, but not beyond.

your puppy's nails every week, taking special care not to cut the "quick" (the central core of blood vessels and nerve endings). In puppies or toys, a scissors type clipper may be easier, whereas in minis or standards, a guillotine nail clipper is usually preferable. The nails are softer after a bath. Most dogs are less sensitive about having their rear nails done, so do these first. Remember the pictures of the village blacksmith shoeing a horse? Hold your dog's feet behind it, so that you are looking at the bottoms of the toenails. You will see a solid core culminating in a hollowed nail. Cut the tip up to the core, but not beyond. One advantage of light-colored nails is that you can see the pink inner core of blood vessels, so this is another clue about where to avoid cutting. Repeat the procedure with the front nails, which tend to grow longer than the rear. Again, if you hold the feet curled behind the leg, dogs seem to accept it better, perhaps because they can't see what you are doing. Don't be surprised if your Eskie, nonetheless, does everything in its power to convince the neighborhood that you are amputating its toes. Speak soothingly, be firm, but don't let a battle ensue. If you must compromise just cut the very tip off and come back later for a shorter cut. Give a reward for good behavior, perhaps after each nail. On occasion you will slip up and cause the nail to bleed. This is best stopped by styptic powder, but if this is not available, dip the nail in flour or hold it to a wet tea bag. Of course your Eskie will take this opportunity to convince you and everyone that will listen that you have, indeed, committed a heinous crime of animal abuse, but the truth is you would be far more abusive to let its nails grow unchecked. When you can hear the pitter-patter of clicking nails, that means that with every step the nails are hitting the floor, and when this happens the bones of the

Many Eskies and owners look forward to grooming sessions as relaxing times of bonding.

foot are spread, causing discomfort and eventually splayed feet and lameness. And if your dog has dewclaws, do not neglect trimming them, as well, because left untrimmed they can get caught on things more easily or actually loop around and grow into the dog's leg.

Stand back and admire your masterpiece. A well-groomed American Eskimo dog is indeed a breathtaking sight. Watch your Adonis strut proudly about the yard, seeming to know that all eyes are upon its magnificent coat. Watch it search out the blackest mud it can find and lie down in it as the crowning step in its beauty makeover. Oh well, good thing the grooming was enjoyable, and besides, remember that Eskies do have a coat that doesn't tend to hold dirt!

Brushing

Begin brushing at the face, moving rearward on one side of the dog, and then the other. If the dog becomes restless, or a mat is difficult to dislodge, move to another area and return to the trouble spot later. Use a pin brush (a brush with wire pins set in a rubber backing) to brush the hair in layers so that it is brushed all the way down to the skin. As your finishing touch, comb all of the long hair backward, from the rear toward the head, so that the hair stands away from the body. For special occasions, some cornstarch in the coat will help it stand out fluffier, but such foreign matter must be brushed completely out of the coat before any dog show competitions.

You may discover some matting behind the ears or behind the elbows, especially during shedding season. The coat is

Brush the coat against the direction of growth to make it stand out from the body. Misting the coat with water before brushing will decrease static and breakage.

60

more prone to mat during shedding season or when it is oily or dirty. Never wash a matted coat, because the mat only becomes more tightly bound. Try to split a mat with your fingers, starting near the skin and pulling it in half longitudinally. Hold the hair between the mat and your dog's skin to avoid painful pulling. More stubborn mats may require splitting with a rake (a wooden brush with hard metal teeth), or as a last resort, scissors. Even with scissors, split the mat into halves, don't just cut it out. To avoid accidentally cutting the skin, wriggle a fine comb between the mat and the skin before you start snipping.

Shedding

An Eskimo dog shedding its coat can best be compared to a field of dandelion puffs in a hurricane. After grooming, you may swear you have an extra Eskie in a garbage bag! Use a slicker brush (a rectangular brush with small, bent wire bristles) to remove loose hair during shedding season. A curved-based slicker is best for really long coats, and a flat-based slicker is best for the medium-length coats that most Eskies have. Shedding can be further hastened by bathing, which seems to loosen the hair follicles. But if shedding is extreme, you could end up with a giant living mat of tangled shed hair after the bath. If you are trying to keep as much coat as possible on your Eskie for as long as possible (for instance, if you wanted it to look its best for a show in two weeks), do not bathe it when it begins shedding.

Among the grooming tools you'll need are (clockwise from bottom left) a slicker brush, pin brush, comb, mat rake, and scissors.

Shedding is controlled not by exposure to warmer temperatures, but by exposure to longer periods of light. This is why indoor dogs, which are exposed to artificial light, tend to shed somewhat all year. In addition, shedding is hormonally controlled in females, such that a shedding period follows each season or a litter of puppies.

Bathing

There is rarely a need for frequent bathing of an Eskimo dog. You will get better results with a shampoo made for dogs. Dog skin has a pH of 7.5, whereas human skin has a pH of 5.5; thus, bathing in a shampoo formulated for the pH of human skin can disrupt the normal pH of dog skin, and lead to scaling and irritation. That's not to say that you can't use human shampoo in a pinch, but if your Eskie has any skin problems, you need to be careful about what shampoo you use. There are many shampoos available that claim to make white coats whiter; the newer ones without bluing are probably easier on your dog's skin. Most shampoos will kill fleas even if not especially formulated as a flea shampoo, but none has any residual killing action on fleas. In addition, there are a variety of therapeutic shampoos for use with skin problems. Dry scaly skin is treated with moisturizing shampoos, excessive

Try to split matted hair with your fingers, starting near the skin and pulling it apart in sections.

scale and dandruff with antiseborrheic shampoos (but be careful here: the tar or selenium sulfide shampoos commonly used for this can stain white fur), damaged skin with antimicrobials (again, iodine-based shampoos can stain), and itchy skin with anti-pruritics (often oatmeal based). Benzoyl peroxide (2.5 to 3 percent), available at your pharmacy, is a good antiseborrhea and antimicrobial shampoo that is safe for white coats. Finally, no one should be without one of the shampoos that requires no water or rinsing. These are wonderful for puppies, emergencies, and last minute foot tidying at shows.

Even the most devoted of owners seldom look forward to bath time. All too often little

Angel Muffin must be dragged to the tub, leaving a trail of doggie skid marks. Once in, the owner must attempt to do the entire bathing process one-handed, because the other is occupied holding the writhing victim as it runs in place and alternately slips down and lunges half out of the tub. Invariably the owner ends up at least as wet as the dog, and certainly in no better mood. In fact, at least the dog is happy when it gets out of the tub; the owner is left to clean up what appears to be major flood damage while the cavorting canine runs outside and plays in the mud. Unfortunately, most owners bring this scenario on themselves through improper early bath training. They put off giving a bath, and when they do, they figure that by making it a thorough bath the results will somehow last longer. The secret is to give lots and lots of tiny baths, so tiny the puppy doesn't have a chance to get scared or tired. If you have a plastic wading pool, your Eskie will practically teach itself to get into water. Rinse (don't even wash) one leg today, the back tomorrow, and so on. Be firm, soothing, and playful. There is no reason a bath should not be a pleasurable experience for both of you.

Once you have worked up to a full-scale bath, begin with a thorough brushing to remove tangles and distribute oils; then wet your dog down, working forward from the rear. Use water that would be comfortable for you to bathe in, and be sure to keep some running on your own hand in order to monitor any temperature changes. Beware

that a fractious Eskie could inadvertently hit a faucet knob and cause itself to be scalded. As long as you keep one hand on your dog's neck or ear, it is less likely to splatter you with a wet dog shake. Once your Eskie's coat is soaked, use your hand or a soft brush to work in the shampoo (it will go a lot farther and be easier to apply if you first mix the shampoo with warm water). Pay special attention to the oily area around the ear base, but avoid getting water in the dog's ears (try plugging with cotton). Rinse thoroughly, this time working from the head back. A creme rinse is

Rinse your Eskie thoroughly, working from the head back to the tail.

seldom necessary, because it tends to make the coat less puffy. Your Eskie will love being towel dried, but be sure not to rub to the point of creating tangles; for special occasions its coat will look its best if you blow it dry while brushing the hair backward. Again, you must accustom your dog to a blow drier gradually, and always keep your hand at the place on the dog you are drying; once your hand gets uncomfortably hot, you know the dog's skin must also be uncomfortable.

A bath may not be fun for your Eskie, but with the proper introduction, it should not be an ordeal either.

This Eskie is all bundled up after its bath.

A well-groomed Eskie is a magnificent sight.

To Good Health

Choosing Your Veterinarian

Do not wait until your puppy gets sick to find a veterinarian. You should choose a veterinarian with as much care as you would your own doctor. Consider availability, facilities, and ability to communicate. You and your veterinarian will form a partnership who will work together to protect your Eskie's health, so your rapport with your veterinarian is very important. Your veterinarian should listen to your observations, and should explain to you exactly what is happening with your Eskie. Ask questions, be sure you understand directions for medications before leaving the office, and be sure that you follow them once you get home. When you take your Eskie to the veterinary clinic, restrain your dog on a leash and do not allow it to mingle with the other patients, who may

Don't wait for an emergency. Find a veterinarian for your Eskie as soon as possible.

be sick or frightened. If you think your dog may have a contagious illness, inform the clinic beforehand so that you can use another entrance. Your veterinarian will be appreciative if your Eskie is clean and under control during his or her examination. Unfortunately, a few poorly bred and trained Eskies have given the breed a poor reputation with some veterinarians: make your Eskie show the doctor otherwise!

Emergencies

Emergencies don't always (in fact, seldom) occur during your veterinarian's office hours. Know the phone number and location of the emergency veterinarian in your area. Make sure you always have enough fuel in your car to make it to the emergency clinic without stopping to find a gas station. Drive carefully and smoothly; if possible have someone else drive while you tend to your dog.

Deciding whether or not you have an emergency can sometimes be difficult. When in doubt, call the veterinarian or emergency clinic. The following situations are all *life threatening emergencies.* For all cases, administer the first aid treatment outlined and seek the nearest veterinary help *immediately.* Call the clinic first so that they can be prepared for your dog when you arrive.

In General

• Make sure breathing passages are open. Loosen the collar and check mouth and throat.
• Be calm and reassuring. A calm dog is less likely to go into shock.

- Move the dog as little and as gently as possible.
- If the dog is in pain, it may bite. Apply a makeshift muzzle with a bandage, belt, or tape. Do not muzzle if breathing difficulties are present.

Shock

Signs: Very pale gums, weakness, unresponsiveness, faint pulse, shivering.

Treatment: Keep the dog warm and calm; control any bleeding; check breathing, pulse, and consciousness and treat these problems if needed.

Heatstroke

Signs: Rapid, loud breathing; abundant thick saliva, bright red mucous membranes, high rectal temperature. Later signs: Unsteadiness, diarrhea, coma.

Treatment: Immediately immerse the dog in cold water at the closest source (tub, lake, pool, gas station hose). If rectal temperature is extremely high (over 106°F [41.1°C]) give a cold water enema. You *must* lower your dog's body temperature quickly (but do not lower it below 100°F [37.8°C]).

Breathing difficulties

Signs: Gasping for breath with head extended, anxiety, weakness; advances to loss of consciousness, bluish tongue (exception: carbon monoxide poisoning causes bright red tongue).

Treatment: If not breathing, give mouth-to-nose respiration:

1. Open the dog's mouth; clear passage of secretions and foreign bodies.
2. Pull the dog's tongue forward; close the dog's mouth; seal the dog's lips with your hand.
3. Seal your mouth over the dog's nose; blow into the dog's nose for three seconds, then release.
4. Continue until the dog breathes on its own.

If due to drowning, turn the dog upside down, holding it by the hind

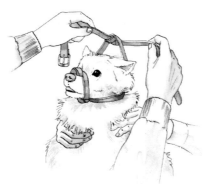

Fashion an emergency muzzle from a belt or clothing to prevent an injured dog from biting. Be sure that breathing is not impaired.

legs, so that water can run out of its mouth. Then administer mouth-to-nose respiration, with the dog's head positioned lower than its lungs.

Bloat

Signs: Restlessness, distended abdomen, gagging, shallow breathing.

Treatment: Get to the nearest veterinarian *at once*. This is a life-threatening emergency; delay can cause irreversible damage and death. Treat for shock en route and monitor breathing.

Move an injured dog as little as possible, and be very gentle and calm when you do.

Poisoning

Signs: Varies according to poison, but commonly include vomiting, convulsions, staggering, collapse.

Treatment: Call your veterinarian and give as much information as possible. Induce vomiting (*except* in the cases outlined below) by giving either hydrogen peroxide, salt water, or mustard and water. Treat for shock and get to the veterinarian at once. Be prepared for convulsions or respiratory distress.

Do *not* induce vomiting if the poison was an acid, alkali, petroleum product, solvent, cleaner, or tranquilizer, or if a sharp object was swallowed; also do *not* induce vomiting if the dog is severely depressed, convulsing, or comatose, or if over two hours have passed since ingestion. If the dog is *not* convulsing or unconscious: Dilute the poison by giving milk, vegetable oil, or egg whites.

Convulsions

Signs: Drooling, stiffness, muscle spasms.

Treatment: Prevent the dog from injuring itself on the furniture or stairs. Remove other dogs from the area. Treat for shock. Contact your veterinarian.

Snakebites

Signs: Swelling, discoloration, pain, fang marks, restlessness, nausea, weakness.

Treatment: Restrain the dog and keep it quiet. Apply a tourniquet between the bite and the heart tight enough to prevent blood from returning to the heart. Make vertical parallel cuts (deep enough for blood to ooze out of) through the fang marks and suction out the blood (do not use your mouth if you have any open sores). Be able to describe the snake if possible so that your veterinarian can have the appropriate treatment ready.

Open Wounds

Signs: Consider wounds to be an emergency if there is profuse bleeding, if extremely deep, if open to chest cavity, abdominal cavity, or head.

Treatment: Control massive bleeding first. Cover the wound with a clean dressing and apply pressure; apply more dressings over the others until bleeding stops. Also elevate the wound site, and apply a cold pack to the site.

If an extremity, apply pressure to the closest pressure point as follows:
• For a front leg: inside of the front leg just above the elbow.
• For a rear leg: inside of the thigh where the femoral artery crosses the thigh bone.
• For the tail: underside of the tail close to where it joins the body.

Use a tourniquet only in life-threatening situations and when all other attempts have failed. Check for signs of shock.

Sucking chest wounds: Place a sheet of plastic or other nonporous material over the hole and bandage it to make an airtight seal.

Abdominal wounds: Place a warm wet sterile dressing over any protruding internal organs; cover with a bandage or towel. Do not attempt to push organs back into the dog.

Head wounds: Apply gentle pressure to control bleeding. Monitor for loss of consciousness or shock and treat accordingly.

Deep Burns

Signs: charred or pearly white skin; deeper layers of tissue exposed.

Treatment: Cool burned area with cool packs, towels soaked in ice water, or by immersing in cold water. If over 50 percent of the dog is burned, do not immerse as this increases the likelihood of shock. Cover with a clean bandage or towel to avoid contamination. Do not apply pressure; do not apply ointments. Monitor for shock.

Electrical Shock

Signs: Collapse, burns inside mouth.

Treatment: Before touching the dog, disconnect the plug or cut power; if that cannot be done immediately, use a wooden pencil, spoon, or broom handle to knock the cord away from the dog. Keep the dog warm and treat for shock. Monitor breathing and heartbeat.

The above list is by no means a complete catalog of emergency situations. Situations not described can usually be treated with the same first aid as for humans. You should maintain a first aid/medical kit for your Eskie, which should contain at least: rectal thermometer, scissors, tweezers, sterile gauze dressings, self-adhesive bandage, instant cold compress, anti-diarrhea medication, ophthalmic ointment, soap, antiseptic skin ointment, hydrogen peroxide, first aid instructions, and veterinarian and emergency clinic numbers.

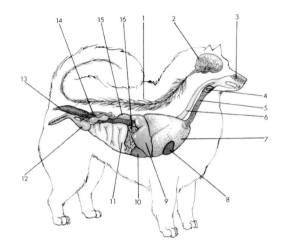

The major internal organs of the American Eskimo dog: 1. spinal cord 2. brain 3. sinus cavity 4. larynx 5. trachea 6. esophagus 7. lung 8. heart 9. liver 10. gall bladder 11. intestine 12. bladder 13. rectum 14. ureter 15. kidney 16. stomach.

Preventative Medicine

The best preventative medicine is that which prevents accidents: a well-trained dog in a well-fenced yard or on a leash, and a properly Eskie-proofed home. Other preventative steps must be taken to avoid diseases and parasites, however.

Vaccinations

Rabies, distemper, leptospirosis, canine hepatitis, parvovirus, and coronavirus are highly contagious and deadly diseases that have broken many a loving owner's heart in the past. Now that vaccinations are available for these diseases one would think they would no longer be a threat, but many dogs remain unvaccinated and continue to succumb to and spread these potentially fatal illnesses. Don't let your Eskie be one of them.

Puppies receive their dam's immunity through nursing in the first two days of life. This is why it is important that your pup's mother be properly immunized before breeding, and that your pup be able to nurse from its dam. This passive immunity gained from the mother will wear off after several weeks, and then the pup will be susceptible to disease unless you provide active immunity through vaccinations. The problem is that there is no way to know exactly when the dam's immunity will wear off, and vaccinations given before that time are ineffective. So you must re-vaccinate over a period of weeks so that your pup will not be unprotected and will receive lasting immunity. Your pup's breeder will have given the first vaccinations to your pup before it was old enough to go home with you. Bring all information about your pup's vaccination history to your veterinarian on your first visit so that the pup's vaccination schedule can be maintained. Meanwhile, it is best not to let your pup mingle with strange dogs.

Health shows—and these two Eskies are perfect pictures of health.

An Eskie's coat is beautiful, but also a wonderful hiding place for many unwelcome guests.

Parasite Control

Intestinal worms: Bring a fresh stool specimen so your veterinarian will check your Eskie for worms when you take the pup to be vaccinated. Most puppies do have worms at some point, even pups from the most fastidious breeders. This is because some types of worms become encysted in the dam's body long before she ever became pregnant; perhaps when she herself was a pup. Here they lie dormant and immune from worming, until hormonal changes due to her pregnancy cause them to be activated, and then they infect her babies. You may be tempted to pick up some worm medication and worm your puppy yourself. Don't. Over-the-counter wormers are largely ineffective and often more dangerous than those available through your veterinarian. Left untreated, worms can cause vomiting, diarrhea, dull coat,

listlessness, anemia, and death. Some heartworm preventatives also prevent most types of intestinal worms, so that if you have a recurring problem in an older puppy or dog they might help.

Tapeworms tend to plague some dogs throughout their lives. There is no preventative, except to diligently rid your Eskie of fleas, because fleas are the intermediate hosts for tapeworms to dogs. Fresh tapeworm segments look like flat, white, one-quarter-inch worms moving on the dog's stool; dried segments look like grains of rice around the dog's anus.

Heartworms: Heartworms are a deadly parasite carried by mosquitoes. Wherever mosquitoes are present, dogs should be on heartworm preventative. There are several types of heartworm preventative on the market; all are effective. Some are also effective in preventing many other types of

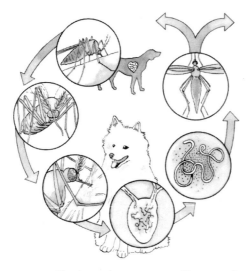

Heartworm larva are spread by mosquitoes from dog to dog. Untreated, they mature and reproduce in the infected dog's heart and can eventually cause death.

worms. Ask your veterinarian when your puppy should begin taking the preventative. If you forget to give the preventative as described, your Eskie may get heartworms. A dog with suspected heartworms should not be given the preventative because a fatal reaction could occur. Heartworms are treatable in their early stages, but the treatment is expensive and not without risks. If untreated, heartworms can kill your Eskie.

Fleas: These bloodsuckers can ruin your Eskie's beautiful coat, make its life miserable, and in some cases even lead to anemia and death. They can be found anywhere on the dog, but prefer the underside and around the tail base. They leave behind a black pepperlike substance (actually flea feces), which turns red upon getting wet. Some Eskies develop an allergic reaction to the saliva of the flea; one bite can cause them to itch and chew for days. Flea allergies are typically characterized by loss of coat

and little red bumps around the lower back and tail base.

Flea control in warm humid areas is the most difficult but still possible. But overzealous and uninformed efforts have often led to the death of pets as well as fleas. Flea insecticides can be categorized as organics, natural pesticides, cholinesterase inhibitors, insect growth regulators, and systemics. Incidentally, the ultrasonic flea repelling collars have been shown to be both ineffective on fleas and irritating to dogs. Scientific studies have also shown that feeding dogs brewer's yeast, as has been advocated for years by many dog owners, is ineffective against fleas.

Organics (e.g., D-Limonene, potassium salts of fatty acids) break down the outer shell of the flea and cause death from dehydration. They are safe, but slow acting and have no residual action. Diatomaceous earth also acts on this same principle; some researchers have expressed concern that breathing its dust can be dangerous to dogs, however. If you choose to use diatomaceous earth, use only natural grade, never pool grade.

Natural pesticides (e.g., Pyrethrin, Permethrin, Rotenone) are relatively safe and kill fleas quickly, but have a

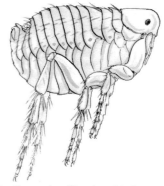

The flea makes life miserable for many pets and owners.

very short residual action. They do not remain in the dog's system and so can be used frequently.

Cholinesterase inhibitors (e.g., Dursban, Diazinon, Malathion, Sevin, Carbaryl, Pro-Spot, Spotton) act on the nervous systems of fleas, dogs, and humans (among others). They are used in yard sprays, dog sprays and dips, flea collars, and systemics. They kill effectively and have fairly good residual action. But they are absorbed into the dog's bloodstream and can poison the dog if overused, and should never be used on puppies or sick dogs. The systemics are drugs that are applied to the dog's skin for absorption into the blood, or given orally, so that the flea dies when it sucks the blood. They, too, are cholinesterase inhibitors. It is extremely important that you be aware of which chemicals in your arsenal are cholinesterase inhibitors. Using a yard spray in conjunction with systemics, or some sprays and dips, or with certain worm medications that are also cholinesterase inhibitors, can be a deadly combination.

Insect growth regulators (IGRs) prevent immature fleas from maturing and have proven to be the most highly effective method for long-term flea control. Precor is the most widely used for indoor applications, but is quickly broken down by ultraviolet light. Fenoxicarb is better for outdoor use because it is resistant to ultraviolet light. IGRs are nontoxic to mammals but tend to be expensive. A new type of IGR on the market are the nematodes that eat flea larva. Studies show them to be effective and safe, but they must be reapplied regularly because they die when their food supply (the current crop of flea larva) is gone.

One final warning. There is a popular product on the market that contains "deet" (diethyl-m-toluamide: the same chemical found in some human insect

A tick before and after feeding.

repellents). It has been implicated in the death of many dogs, including a beloved Eskie show dog.

Because only about 1 percent to 10 percent of your home's flea population is actually on your dog, you must concentrate on treating your home and yard. These are best treated with a combination adult flea killer and IGR. Wash all pet bedding and vacuum other surfaces regularly, and especially before applying insecticides. Be sure that sprays reach into small crevices. Outside, cut grass short and spray in all areas except those that are never shaded (fleas do not mature in these areas).

Although it is seldom desirable to shave an Eskie, it may be of help if you are fighting a battle with fleas. You can then use a flea comb for daily control of fleas on your dog, and flea sprays and powders can penetrate the coat better.

It may not be easy, but you can win the battle. Every time you feel like giving up, consider how your Eskie deserves to live: free of the constant itching caused by a colony of blood-sucking parasites.

Ticks: Ticks are also a pesky disease-carrying pest. Rocky Mountain spotted fever, Lyme disease, and, most commonly, "tick fever" (erlichiosis) are potentially fatal diseases carried by

Visiting a sick friend in the hospital?

ticks. Ticks most often attach around the ears and neck area, but may also be found hiding between your Eskie's toes. Use a tissue or tweezers to remove ticks, because some diseases can be transmitted to humans. Kill the tick first with alcohol, if desired. Then pull slowly and steadily, trying not to leave the head in the dog. If the head is left in, keep an eye on the area to make sure an infection does not result. Do not attempt to burn the tick out; you may set fire to your Eskie!

Ear mites: Tiny but irritating, ear mites are highly communicable and often found in puppies. Affected dogs will shake their head, scratch their ears, and carry their head sideways. There is a dark waxy buildup in the ear canal, usually of both ears. If you place some of this wax on a piece of dark paper, and have very good eyes, you may be able to see tiny white moving specks. These are the culprits. Although there are over-the-counter ear mite preparations, they can cause

worse irritation. Therefore, ear mites should be diagnosed and treated by your veterinarian.

Mange mites: Dogs are prone to two very different forms of mange. Sarcoptic mange is highly contagious to dogs and humans. Characterized by intense itching and often scaling of the ear tips, it is easily treated with insecticidal dips. Demodectic mange is not contagious and does not itch, but can be difficult to cure. It tends to run in families, and is characterized by a moth-eaten appearance, often on the face or feet; advanced cases lead to serious secondary staphylococcal infections. Some localized forms may go away on their own, but more widespread cases will need a special dip regime prescribed by your veterinarian. You must adhere to the dip schedule fanatically in order to effect a cure in these cases.

Dental Care

At around four to five months of age, your Eskie puppy will begin to shed its

An Eskie is vulnerable to illness and injury the same way as its owner. Be on the lookout for symptoms, and consult your veterinarian when necessary.

baby teeth and show off new permanent teeth. Sometimes baby teeth, especially the canines, are not shed, so that the permanent tooth grows in beside the baby tooth. If this condition persists for over a week, consult your veterinarian. Retained baby teeth can cause misalignment of adult teeth. Check the way your puppy's teeth match up; in a correct bite, the bottom incisors should touch the back of the top incisors when the mouth is closed. Deviations from this can cause chewing problems and discomfort.

Hard dog foods and chew bones are not adequate for preventing tartar. You should brush your dog's teeth once or twice weekly with a child's toothbrush and dog toothpaste. You can also rub the teeth with hydrogen peroxide or a baking soda solution on a gauze pad to help remove tartar. Thicker tartar deposits will have to be removed with a dental scraper by your veterinarian, possibly under anesthesia. Thick tartar can lead to bad breath, tooth loss, periodontal disease, abscessed roots, and even heart problems.

Common Ailments and Symptoms

Coughing

Any persistent cough should be checked by your veterinarian. Coughing irritates the throat and can lead to secondary infections if allowed to continue unchecked. There are many reasons for coughing, including allergies, but two of the most common are kennel cough and heart disease.

Kennel cough: This is a highly communicable airborne disease against which you can also request your dog be vaccinated. This is an especially good idea if you plan to have your dog around other dogs at training classes, while being boarded, or if your Eskie meets a lot of other dogs on walks.

Unfortunately, there is no vaccination to prevent heart disease. In an older dog, especially following exercise or in the evening, coughing is often the first indication an owner has of heart disease. Treatment with diuretics prescribed by your veterinarian can help alleviate the coughing for awhile.

Vomiting

Vomiting is a not uncommon occurrence that may or may not indicate a serious problem. You should consult your veterinarian immediately if your dog vomits a foul substance resembling fecal matter (indicating a blockage in the intestinal tract), blood (partially digested blood resembles coffee grounds), or if there is projectile vomiting, in which the stomach contents are forcibly ejected up to a distance of several feet. Sporadic vomiting with poor appetite and generally poor condition could indicate worms or a more serious internal disease that should also be checked by your veterinarian.

Overeating is a common cause of vomiting in puppies, especially if they follow eating with playing. Feed smaller meals more frequently if this becomes a problem. Vomiting after eating grass is common and usually of no great concern. Repeated vomiting could indicate that the dog has eaten spoiled food, indigestible objects, or may have stomach illness. Use the same home treatment as that outlined for diarrhea below.

Diarrhea

Diarrhea can result from overexcitement or nervousness, a change in diet or water, sensitivity to certain foods, overeating, intestinal parasites, infectious diseases such as parvovirus or coronavirus, or ingestion of spoiled food or toxic substances. Bloody diarrhea, diarrhea with vomiting, fever, or other signs of toxicity, or a diarrhea that lasts for more than a day should not be allowed to continue without veterinary advice.

Less severe diarrhea can be treated at home by withholding or severely restricting food and water. Ice cubes can be given to satisfy thirst. Administer a human anti-diarrheal medicine that does not contain aspirin; use the same weight dosage as recommended for humans. A bland diet consisting of rice (flavored if need be with cooked, drained hamburger), cottage cheese, or cooked macaroni should be given for several days.

Urinary Tract Diseases

If your dog drinks and urinates more than usual, it may be suffering from a kidney problem. See your veterinarian for a proper diagnosis and treatment. Although the excessive urination may cause problems in keeping your house clean or your night's sleep intact, *never* try to restrict water from a dog with kidney disease. Untreated kidney disease can lead to death.

Note: Increased thirst and urination could also be a sign of *diabetes*.

If your dog has difficulty or pain in urination, urinates suddenly but in small amounts, or passes cloudy or bloody urine, it may be suffering from a problem of the bladder, urethra, or prostate. Your veterinarian will need to examine your Eskie to determine the exact nature of the problem. Bladder infections must be treated promptly to avoid the infection reaching the kidneys. A common cause of urinary incontinence in older spayed females is lack of estrogen, which can be treated. Your veterinarian should check your older (intact) male's prostate to ensure that it is not overly enlarged, which can cause problems in both urination and defecation.

Impacted Anal Sacs
Dogs have two anal sacs that are normally emptied by rectal pressure during defecation. Sometimes they fail to empty properly and become impacted or infected. Constant licking of the anus or scooting of the anus along the ground are characteristic signs of anal sac impaction. This is an uncomfortable condition for your dog and should not be left unattended. Your veterinarian (or most dog groomers) can show you how to empty the anal sacs yourself.

Eye Discharge
A watery discharge, accompanied by squinting or pawing, often indicates a foreign body in the eye. Examine under the lids and use a moist cotton swab to remove any debris. Flooding the eye with ophthalmic irrigating or saline solution can also aid in removal. After removal, put some antibiotic ophthalmic ointment in the inner corner of the eye. If your dog still shows discomfort, you will need to have your pet's doctor take a look. Continued tearing of the eye could be due to eyelid anomalies that irritate the cornea; if ignored, they could injure the eye to the point of

The Health Check
It may seem like there are a lot of things that can go wrong with your beloved friend. But you can do your part by looking for early signs of problems and reporting any concerns to your veterinarian. A weekly health check should be part of your grooming procedure. The health check should include:
• Examining the eyes for discharge or cloudiness.
• Examining the ears for bad smell, redness, or discharge.
• Examining the mouth for red swollen gums, loose teeth, or bad breath.
• Examining the skin for parasites, hair loss, or lumps.
• Observing your dog for signs of lameness or incoordination, or for behavioral changes.
• Keeping a record of your Eskie's weight because weight changes may not be noticeable under that thick coat.
• Taking your Eskie to your veterinarian for a yearly checkup.
• Taking your older pet for checkups even more frequently.

causing blindness. However, many Eskies tear for no discernable reason.

A thick or crusty discharge suggests conjunctivitis. Mild cases can be treated by over-the-counter preparations for humans, but if you don't see improvement within a day of treatment, your veterinarian should be consulted.

Any time your dog's pupils do not react to light or when one eye reacts differently from another, take your Eskie to the veterinarian immediately. It could indicate a serious ocular or neurological problem.

Skin and Coat Problems
Itchy skin most often results from flea infestation, sarcoptic mange, or aller-

A healthy dog is a relaxed dog, even when surrounded by the stimulating colors of a bright afghan.

gies (to food, airborne particles, grass, or flea saliva). First make sure that not a single flea is on your dog. If scratching continues, you and your veterinarian will have to play detectives. Mange mites can be detected through skin scrapings; for allergies, you can try avoiding certain foods and environments. Often a lamb and rice-based food will bring relief. New carpeting or wet grass may be the culprit. Cortisone can bring some relief from the itching, but can cause damage to your Eskie in the long run if used too frequently.

In some cases, hair is lost without the dog itching. Demodectic mange, thyroid deficiency, estrogen excess, ringworm, and seborrhea are all possibilities that your veterinarian can diagnose.

Blisters and brown crust on the stomach of your Eskimo puppy indicate puppy impetigo. Clean the area

twice daily with dilute hydrogen peroxide or surgical soap, and treat with a topical antibiotic.

Most bumps and lumps are not cause for concern, but because there is always a possibility of cancer, they should be examined by your veterinarian. This is especially true of a sore that does not heal, or any pigmented lump that begins to grow or bleed.

Limping

Puppies are especially susceptible to bone and joint injuries, and should not be encouraged to jump off of high places, walk on their hind legs, or run until exhausted. Persistent limping in puppies may result from one of several developmental bone problems, and should be checked. Both puppies and adults should be kept off of slippery floors that could cause them to

Watch for signs of lameness in your Eskie. It can be due to several causes and should be treated immediately.

lose their footing. Limping may or may not indicate a serious problem. When associated with extreme pain, fever, swelling, discoloration, deformity, or grating or popping sounds, you should have your veterinarian examine your Eskie at once. Ice packs may help minimize swelling if applied immediately after an injury. Fractures should be immobilized by splinting above and below the site of fracture (rolled magazines work well on legs) before moving the dog. Mild lameness should be treated by complete rest; if it still persists after two days, your dog will need to be examined by its doctor. Knee injuries are common in dogs; most do not get well on their own. Avoid pain medications that might encourage the use of an injured limb. In older dogs, or dogs with a previous injury, limping is often the result of arthritis. This condition can be treated with aspirin, but should be done so only under veterinary supervision.

Medications

Giving medications to your Eskie should not be difficult. For pills, open your dog's mouth and place (don't throw) the pill well to the back and in the middle of the tongue. Close the mouth and gently stroke the throat until your dog swallows. Beware that capsules often stick to the tongue or roof of the mouth; pre-wetting them or covering them with cream cheese or some other food may help. For liquid medicine, tilt the head back and place the liquid in the pouch of the cheek. Then close your dog's mouth until it swallows. Always give the full course of medications prescribed by your veterinarian.

You may also need to take your dog's temperature on occasion. Use a rectal thermometer, preferably the digital type, lubricate it, and insert it about 2 inches (5.1 cm) (less in a smaller Eskie). Do not allow your dog to sit down, or the thermometer could break. Normal temperature is 100.5 to 102.5°F (38.1–39.2°C).

When You Must Say Good-bye

Unfortunately, there comes the time when, no matter how diligent you have been, neither you nor your veterinarian can prevent your Eskie from succumbing to old age or an incurable illness. It seems hard to believe that you will have to say good-bye to someone who has been such a focal point of your life—in truth, a real member of your family. That dogs live such a short time compared to humans is a cruel fact, and as much as you may wish otherwise, your Eskie is a dog and is not immortal. You should realize that both of you have been fortunate to have shared so many good times, but make sure that your Eskie's remaining time is still pleasurable.

Many terminal illnesses make your dog feel very bad, and there comes a point where your desire to keep your friend with you as long as possible may not be the kindest thing for either of you. Ask your veterinarian if there is a reasonable chance of your dog getting better, and if he or she thinks your dog is suffering. Ask yourself if your dog is getting pleasure out of life, and if it enjoys most of its days. If your Eskie no longer eats its dinner or treats, this is a sign that it does not feel well and you must face the prospect of doing what is best for your beloved friend. Euthanasia is painless and involves giving an overdose of an anesthetic. If your dog is scared of the vet's office, you might feel better having the doctor meet you at home or come out to your car. Although it won't be easy, try to remain with your Eskie so that your pet's last moments will be filled with your love. Try to recall the wonderful times you have shared and realize that however painful it is losing such a once-in-a-lifetime dog, it is better than never having had such a friend in the first place.

Having Fun with Your American Eskimo Dog

So far, it might sound as though all that's involved in owning a dog is a whole lot of work. But millions of people would not own dogs if that were *all* there was to it! For every moment of work, there are manyfold more moments of love and fun! You don't need a book to tell you how to love your dog, but there are some helpful hints when it comes to having fun with your dog.

The Great Outdoors—Safely

Walking the dog—such a simple task that can bring such tranquility or such aggravation, because, as with anything else, there is a right way, and a wrong way, to do it. If you are walking around the neighborhood, use a collar that will not slip over your Eskie's head, a 6-foot (1.8 m) non-chain leash, or a longer retractable leash. Hold the leash firmly, keep your eyes open for marauding canines and enticing felines, and never allow so much loose lead that your dog could suddenly jump in the path of a passing vehicle. An astounding number of dogs get hit by cars while on a lead because their owners neglected to be prepared for the unexpected.

Pick a regular time of day to walk and try to stick to it. Your Eskie will come to expect a walk at this time and won't fall for any of your excuses. Walk briskly so that you both can get a good workout, but not too briskly for the littler Eskies. A trotting pace is usually best. If you wish your dog to jog with you, remember that dogs need to be worked up to long dis-

tances gradually, and again, be considerate of the mini and toy Eskies. Check the footpads regularly for signs of abrasion, foreign bodies, tears, or blistering. Hot pavement can blister a dog's feet. Finally, leave your dog at home in hot weather. Dogs are unable to cool themselves through sweating, and heatstroke in jogging dogs is a common emergency seen by veterinarians in the summer.

You may be lucky enough to have a place to allow your Eskie to run off-leash. Never allow your friend to run loose in sight of traffic. Although your dog may usually stay with you, keep in mind that a cat, rabbit, or other dogs

Eskie heaven is rolling around in the grass with your owner.

Eskies love to walk, even in the snow. This little Eskie tackles its first snowfall.

can lure your dog away and cause it to end up in potentially dangerous places. Never unhook the lead until you know everything about the area in which you will be walking. Is there a roadway around the next bend in the path? Dogs have been killed or injured running off of unseen cliffs, carried away by fast moving water in drainage culverts, and even eaten by alligators. Watch out for strange dogs; some may not be friendly, and a little Eskie is no match for many of them. Once you know your area, be prepared for many wonderful times watching your little wolf in sheep's clothing feel the call of the wild. Few things in life rival the look of sheer ecstasy in an Eskie's eyes as it reverts back to its roots and romps with unbridled enthusiasm though nature.

You may fear that with such joy your dog may be overcome with the call of the wild and run away. Probably not. But for insurance, you should have practiced letting your dog run loose in enclosed areas such as ball fields, and practiced the "come" com-mand and used treats to ensure that your dog came every single time. You may even want to make sure that your dog is already hungry (and maybe a little tired) before you go if you have any doubts about its eager return.

Be sure that you pack some water and a little bowl for your dog. Also pack tape and bandages in case of a cut footpad—either that or plan on carrying your lame companion all the way home. There may, in fact, be some recreation that Eskies like better than hiking; however, it has yet to be discovered.

In the Public Eye

Hitting the Road

The small size, easy going demeanor, and desire to be by their owner's side make Eskimo dogs a natural traveling companion. You may find that sharing a trip with your Eskie, especially if you would otherwise be traveling alone, can be a rewarding experience. But do consider that trav-eling with any dog sets limits on where

Eskies find security when traveling in the familiarity and safety of their cage.

you can go. Many motels do not accept pets, and many attractions have no facilities for temporary pet boarding. Most beaches, and many state parks, do not allow dogs. Dogs can no longer travel on trains. There are several publications listing motels that do accept dogs (e.g., *Touring with Towser*, a directory published by Gaines Dog Food Company) and many major attractions do have dog boarding facilities on their grounds. Be sure to call ahead and quiz them about their safety precautions. A chain next to the highway, for example, simply will not do.

Sometimes the rules against dogs seem so very unfair. Unfortunately, in many cases they are the only self-defense establishments have against irresponsible dog owners. Wherever you go, you will be scrutinized and upheld as an example of a typical dog owner. Don't let your dog defecate wherever it pleases. Look for an appropriate route to walk your dog, then clean up after it. Don't leave your dog alone in a motel room. Loneliness and a strange room may cause your dog to bark, howl, or destroy the furniture. Don't let your dog chase wildlife at parks. Instead, go out of your way to do things properly, and perhaps, slowly, the tide may once turn again in favor of pets on the road.

An Eskie's luggage should include an airline-approved cage.

Luckily there still remain some places where pets are welcome. Schedule several stops in places your Eskie can enjoy. If you are driving, bring a long retractable lead so your dog can stretch its legs safely every few hours along the way. Keep an eye out for little nature excursions, which are wonderful for refreshing both dog and owner. But always do so with a cautious eye—never risk your or your dog's safety by stopping in totally desolate locales, no matter how breathtaking the view. Never let your Eskie off-lead in an unfamiliar spot.

Ideally your Eskie should always ride with the equivalent of a doggy seat belt: the cage. Many dogs have emerged from their cages shaken but safe, from accidents that would have otherwise proved fatal. A cage can also help prevent accidents if you have an Eskie that thinks it should be driving. A cage with a padlocked door can also be useful when you need to leave the dog in the car with the windows down.

You will need an airline-approved cage if your Eskie would rather travel by air. Most Eskies will have to fly in a pressurized baggage compartment, but some small toy Eskies may be able to ride in the passenger section. Talk at length to an airline representative about facilities and requirements when you make reservations for yourself and your dog. Airlines will not generally accept dogs to be flown in extreme temperature conditions. Flying dogs is relatively safe, but not entirely without risk, usually from overheating. It is preferable to fly with your dog as excess baggage than it is to ship it alone. If you must ship it by itself, it is better shipped "counter-to-counter" than as regular air cargo. In hot weather, it is best to have the dog fly at night, and it is always best to avoid plane changes, which expose dogs to weather conditions, extra

stress, and the possibility of being misrouted. Make sure the cage is secure, and for good measure put an elastic bungee band around the cage door. Plaster your name and address all over the cage. Don't feed your dog before traveling. The cage should have a small dish that can be attached to the door. The night before the trip fill it with water and freeze it; as it melts during the flight, the dog will have water that otherwise would have spilled out during the loading process. Also include a large chew bone to occupy your jet-setter. Be sure to line the cage with soft, absorbent material, preferably something that can be thrown away if soiled. The flight crew of the plane should have been alerted to the fact that a dog is traveling, but it never hurts to remind the flight attendant. When you arrive at your destination find out where to meet your friend; if flying excess baggage, your dog typically will arrive a little after the last of the regular baggage is distributed, but it is against regulations for live animals to be placed on the baggage carousels. If your dog has not arrived by five minutes after the last baggage from your flight, inquire; if need be, become demanding. But in most cases bring your leash and be prepared for a joyous reunion! And once again, remember, the public's eyes are upon you, so make sure your Eskie is a perfect lady or gentleman at the airport.

Whether you will be spending your nights at a motel, campground, or even a friend's home, always have your dog on its very best behavior. Ask beforehand if it will be OK for you to bring your Eskie. Have your dog clean and parasite-free. Do not allow your Eskie pal to run loose at motels or campgrounds, and do not allow it to run helter-skelter through the homes of friends. Bring your dog's own clean blanket or bed, or better yet, its cage. Your Eskie will appreciate the familiar place to sleep. Even though your dog may be used to sleeping on furniture at home, a proper guest stays on the floor when visiting. Walk and walk your dog (and clean up after it) to make sure no accidents occur inside. If they do, clean them immediately. Don't leave any surprises for your hosts! Never, never leave your dog unattended in a strange place. The dog's perception is that you have left and forgotten it; it either barks or tries to dig its way out through the doors and windows in an effort to find you, or becomes upset and relieves itself on the carpet. Always remember that those who allow your dog to spend the night are doing so with a certain amount of trepidation; make sure your Eskie is so well behaved that they invite both of you back.

You will need to pack a little suitcase for your dog as well as yourself, which should include your first aid kit, a bowl, some dog biscuits and chewies, flea spray, flea comb, a brush, a change of bedding, short and long leashes, and food. Besides the regular tags, your dog should wear identification indicating where you could be reached while on your trip or including the address of someone you know will be at home. If you are traveling by car, a jug of water from home can be a big help, as many dogs are very sensitive to changes in water and can develop diarrhea.

It may sound like a lot of work, but with a little preparation your Eskie can become a seasoned world traveler, and you may wonder how you ever hit the road without your travel companion before.

The Canine Good Citizen

Even if the only trip you take with your Eskie is around the block, please, for the sake of dog ownership in the future, maintain the same high standards that you would if traveling.
• Always clean up after your dog. Carry a little plastic bag for disposal later.
• Don't let your dog run loose where it could bother picnickers, bicyclists, joggers, or children.
• Never let your dog bark unchecked.
• Never let your dog jump up on people.

In order to formally recognize dogs that behave in public, the AKC offers the Canine Good Citizen (CGC) certificate. To pass this test, all your Eskie must demonstrate is that it is well mannered in public. This means that it will walk quietly with you through a crowd, sit for examination, not jump up on, act aggressively toward, or shy from someone who greets you, and stay in place without barking. The CGC is perhaps the most important title that your Eskie can earn. The most magnificent champion in the show ring is no credit to its breed if it is not a good public citizen in the real world.

Whether walking your Eskie around your block or in a strange neighborhood or roadside rest stop, always clean up afterward.

The American Eskimo Dog Association Christmas Team visits a local nursing home.

The Good Samaritan

Therapy Dogs

As more of the population becomes elderly and either unable to care for or keep a pet, the result is particularly sad for lonely people who may have relied upon the companionship of a pet throughout most of their independent years. Studies have shown that pet ownership increases life expectancy and petting animals can lower blood pressure. In recent years, nursing home residents and hospitalized children have come to look forward to visits by dogs and other pets. These dogs must be meticulously well mannered and well groomed; to be registered as a Certified Therapy Dog a dog must demonstrate that it will act in an obedient, outgoing, gentle manner to strangers. With their irresistible baby harp seal faces and friendly yet unassuming demeanor, the Eskie is a natural for this enjoyable and rewarding task, and several Eskies have already proven themselves to be excellent breed ambassadors.

Search and Rescue

Have you ever dreamed of saving a life? With the aid of your Eskimo dog, you could be somebody's hero. In fact, an Eskimo dog is ideally suited for this crucial work. Locating lost children, earthquake victims, and even buried or drowning victims are all in a hard day's work for a search and rescue dog.

This Eskie has been trained as a search and rescue dog.

These dogs must be taught to use their noses to track or sniff out people; they must be agile enough to work in demolished areas, and small enough to fit into small crevices. An added attribute is that a rescue dog should be friendly and friendly looking, so that any children it finds will not be frightened. Although this sounds like a description of the Eskimo dog, only a few have yet taken up this heroic challenge.

Showing Off

Mind Games

Although sitting and staying and the like are necessary for good manners, they don't exactly astound your friends. For that you need something flashy, some incredible feat of intelligence and dexterity—a dog trick. Try the standards: roll over, play dead, catch, sit up, jump the stick, speak. All are easy to teach with the help of the same obedience concepts outlined in the training section (beginning on page 38).They are very fun to teach because they usually are taught with the aid of treats. For example, to catch a treat, toss a morsel in the air above your dog's nose. When it hits the ground, pick it up. Eventually your Eskie will figure out that it will have to grab the food before you do, and will snatch it up before it lands. The variety of tricks is limitless, but you will find that your particular dog is more apt to perform in ways that make some tricks easier than others to teach. Most Eskies are easy to teach to "speak"; wait until it appears your dog will bark, say "speak," and then reward with a treat after the bark. A dog that likes to lie on its back is a natural for "roll over"; give the command when the dog is already on its back, then guide the dog the rest of the way over (and eventually over and over) with a treat. If your dog can physically do it, you can teach it when

to do it. Performing tricks enabled the American Eskimo dog to work its way into American homes and hearts in the first place; today, Eskies don't need to be under a circus tent to work the same magic.

Obedience Trials

Some people don't like to compete at anything, and others aren't happy unless everything is a contest. With obedience trials, both types can be satisfied.

You plan on training your Eskie the commands heel, sit, down, come, and stay for use in everyday life. Add the "stand for exam" (also useful in everyday life, for example, at the veterinarian's), and your dog will have the basic skills necessary to earn the AKC Companion Dog (CD) title. Specifically, the AKC CD title requires the dog to:

1. Heel on-lead, sitting automatically each time you stop; negotiating right, left, and about turns without guidance from you; and changing to a faster and slower pace.

2. Heel in a figure eight around two people, still on-lead.

3. Stand still off-lead while a judge touches it while you are 6 feet (1.8 m) away.

4. Do the exercises in number 1, except off-lead.

5. Come to you when called from 20 feet (6 m) away, and then return to the heel position on command.

6. Stay in a sitting position with a group of other dogs, while you are 20 feet (6 m) away, for one minute.

7. Stay in a down position with the same group while you are 20 feet (6 m) away, for three minutes.

Each exercise has points assigned to it, and points are deducted for the inevitable imperfections. In all but the heel commands, you can give a command only one time, period, and in no cases can you touch, speak to, physically guide, correct, praise, or do anything except give the dog's name, followed by the command during that exercise. No food can be carried into the ring. You must pass each individual exercise and earn above the minimal 170 points to qualify. To earn the degree, you must qualify three times. The UKC Companion Dog title (U-CD) requires much the same exercises, with the biggest difference being that one dog is required to stay in the ring on a down/stay while another is doing its individual exercise.

Can you teach an old dog new tricks? Yes! Just ask the owner of the Eskie that started to compete in obedience at age 13—and showed up the youngsters! With an Eskie at your side, you already have an unfair advantage. Don't be surprised or embarrassed if you make more errors and lose more points than your Eskie does; your Eskie will forgive you. Joining an obedience club will introduce you to others who will be glad to give you training pointers and won't hesitate to tell you that you have two left feet. If you enter competition with your Eskie, remember this as your golden rule: Companion Dog means just that; failing a trial, in the scope of life, is an insignificant event. Getting mad at, or being disappointed in, your dog defeats the purpose of obedience as a way of promoting a harmonious partnership between trainer and dog. Never let a ribbon or a few points become more important than a trusting relationship with your companion.

In both AKC and UKC there are more advanced titles, where everything is done off-lead. The Companion Dog Excellent (CDX or U-CDX) also requires retrieving and jumping, and the even more advanced Utility Dog (UD or U-UD) requires hand signals and scent discrimination. Even with an Eskimo dog, these titles take years of work; a UD is a rarity in any breed.

With their circus heritage, Eskies are natural trick performers.

The AKC Obedience Trial Champion (OTCH) degree is given only to dogs with UDs that outscore many other UD dogs in many, many trials. If you are at an obedience trial and see that an OTCH dog of any breed is entered, take the time to watch it go through its paces. At this writing, there is no OTCH American Eskimo dog. Could yours be the first?

Tracking

The dog's sense of smell is one of its most awe-inspiring attributes. Although the Eskie is not usually regarded as a scenting or tracking dog, it nonetheless has an acute sense of smell and is capable of following a trail with the tenacity of a bloodhound—you just have to show your Eskie that you want it to. Several books are available describing the training of a tracking dog; suffice it to say here that it takes devotion to the cause and an affinity for waking up early. If you would like to test the

A standard Eskie practices the seesaw on an agility course.

waters, you can evaluate your Eskie's propensity to use its nose by hiding dog biscuits around the house or yard and then having your Eskie sniff them out. This is the basis for one popular method of training: treats are dropped every few feet along a trail laid by the owner (or other tracklayer), and the dog is encouraged to find them. The dog gradually learns that by following the trail it will come across hidden treasures. Eventually fewer and fewer treats are used, but there is the mother lode of dog biscuits awaiting at the end of the trail. Tracking aficionados are perhaps the most devoted of dog trainers, and enjoy the solitude of spending the morning alone with their special dog. Dogs that pass an AKC sanctioned test are awarded the titles Tracking Dog (TD) and the more advanced Tracking Dog Excellent (TDX). Again, as of this writing, the Eskie world awaits its first recipient of these titles.

Agility

Perhaps no competitive event available for Eskies is more suited for this versatile breed, and certainly none is more loved by the dogs! Agility combines obedience, athleticism, and quickness, and is best suited for a medium-sized dog. Sound like any breed you know? Dogs must negotiate a course of obstacles and jumps, including an A-frame, seesaw, elevated boardwalk, tunnels, and a variety of high and broad jumps (adjusted according to the height of the dog). There are Novice, Open, and Excellent classes, and the AKC awards, in increasing level of difficulty, the titles Novice Agility Dog (NAD), Open Agility Dog (OAD), Agility Dog Excellent (ADE), and Master Agility Excellent (MAX).

As a comparatively new sport, you may have difficulty finding a group with which to train, but you can practice some of the elements on your own.

A standard and two miniatures compete at a UKC conformation show.

Children's playgrounds or your own living room can be used as practice arenas. Some resourceful trainers have used a dozen plumber's helpers as weaving poles (ignoring the questioning looks of the people watching them buy them!) or a line of chairs with a sheet draped over them as a tunnel. With their circus star–studded pedigrees, there is perhaps no sport more ideally suited for the American Eskimo dog.

Flyball and Scent Hurdles

Both of these are relay races run with teams of four dogs that run down a course of four small jumps. In scent hurdle competition, the dog must then choose which of several articles belongs to its owner, and return with the correct one. Flyball competition also involves a course of jumps, but at the end of the course the dog then presses a treadle that pops a ball out of a box, catches the ball, and returns with it on the run to its owner. One of

the dogs on the world record-setting flyball team just so happens to be an American Eskimo dog!

Conformation

There is something about dog owners that inevitably leads to the assertation that "my dog's better than your dog" and dog shows must be the result of this quirk of human nature. Conformation shows evaluate your Eskimo dog in comparison to the official breed standard. The judge will examine each dog from the tip of its nose to the tip of its tail, feeling its body structure beneath its coat, studying its way of moving, and looking at the total picture it creates. If you find yourself admiring your dog as it struts and poses around the yard, you may be interested in showing off at a conformation show. The best place to start is by getting an honest opinion from your dog's breeder. As long as your Eskie has no disqualifying faults, you can show it. Of course, you may not win, but you will still learn a lot about the show world and be better prepared in the event that you would like to show your next Eskimo dog.

Assuming that you want to take the plunge, you will need to train your Eskie to pose and trot. The correct show pose is with all four paws pointing straight forward, legs parallel to each other and perpendicular to the ground, tail over the back, head and ears up. If your dog already knows the stand for exam, you have a head start. Reward the dog for keeping its feet where you place them, and for looking alert. In AKC shows you can use "bait" (typically boiled liver) to get the dog's attention in the ring, but even carrying bait into the show ring is against the rules at UKC shows. Practice trotting in a dead straight line, and encourage your dog to trot (not gallop!) in a lively animated fashion. A happy attitude will overshadow a myriad of faults! The most common mistake new handlers make is to demand their dogs stand like statues for so long the poor dogs become bored, and then they wonder why the dog hates to show. There are professional handlers who will show your dog for you and probably win more often than

A judge checks this Eskie from the tip of its nose to the tip of its tail as part of the conformation competition.

you would; however, there is nothing like the thrill of winning when you are on the other end of the lead!

Contact your local kennel club or even obedience club and find out if they have handling classes, or when the next match will be held. Matches are informal events where everybody is learning: puppies, handlers, even the judges. Win or lose, never take one judge's opinion too seriously, and no matter how obviously feebleminded the judge is, be polite and keep your comments to yourself.

Of course, your Eskie must be groomed to perfection, and you should get a show lead, which is much thinner than your regular leash and collar. You, too, must be groomed (you don't want to embarrass your Eskie). For shows, proper attire is a sports jacket for men, a skirt with flat shoes for women. At matches, the dress code is less formal.

At a real AKC show, each time a judge chooses your dog as the best dog of its sex that is not already a Champion it wins up to five points, depending upon how many dogs it defeats. To become an AKC Champion your Eskie must win 15 points including two majors (defeating enough dogs to win three to five points at a time). You may enter any class for which your dog is eligible: Puppy, Novice, American Bred, Bred by Exhibitor, or Open. The Best of Breed or Best of Variety classes are for dogs that are already Champions. Before entering, you should contact the AKC and ask for the rules and regulations concerning dog shows, which will explain the requirements for each class. Your dog must be entered about three weeks before the show date, and you will need to get a premium list and entry form from the appropriate show superintendent (their addresses are available from the AKC or most dog magazines).

At a UKC show, the atmosphere is considerably more relaxed than at AKC shows. Unlike AKC shows, UKC shows can be entered the morning of the show; there are no superintendents, and all of the information necessary to enter can be found in the UKC publication *Bloodlines*. You must bring the dog's registration certificate and pedigree to enter. The requirements for a championship, too, are somewhat different. First of all, 100 points are needed. Classes for non-champions are divided by age, sex, and variety, and the winner of each class receives five points, regardless of the number of dogs defeated. If it then wins best of its sex in that variety, it wins eight more points; best of its sex overall wins another ten points, and finally, best overall wins yet 12 more points. Once dogs become champions, they can compete against each other to earn the prestigious Grand Champion title.

To survive as a conformation competitor, you must be able to separate your own ego and self-esteem from your dog; many people cannot do this. You must also not allow your dog's ability to win in the ring cloud your perception of your dog's true worth in its primary role: that of friend and companion.

Your Eskie never has to step foot in a show ring, earn a title, or thrill anyone except you to be the Grand Champion of your heart. Whatever you consider to be fun, your little friend will agree with. Whether sitting beside you watching TV, sneaking a snack under the table, or strolling down the beach at dawn, your Eskie will be "esktatic" because it is doing it with you.

This beautiful Eskie is a winner, both at shows and relaxing in the backyard.

The American Eskimo Dog Standard

Every breed has a blueprint: a description of the ideal specimen. No one dog ever fits that blueprint perfectly, but at the very least a dog should fit the standard well enough so that it is easily recognized as an American Eskimo dog. This possession of breed attributes is known as type, and is an important requirement of any Eskie. A dog should also be built in such a way that it can go about its daily life with minimal exertion and absence of lameness. This equally important attribute is known as soundness. Add to these the attributes of good health and temperament, and you have the four cornerstones of the ideal American Eskimo dog.

The Ideal American Eskimo Dog

Although the UKC standard and the AKC standard are worded differently, their essence is the same, with only a few areas of discrepancy. The largest discrepancy concerns the classification of sizes. UKC recognizes only two sizes: miniatures (males 12 to 15 inches [30.5–38.1 cm] inclusive and females 11 to 14 inches [27.9–35.6 cm] inclusive) and standards (males over 15 up to 19 inches [38.1–48.3 cm] and females over 14 up to 18 inches [35.6–45.7 cm]).The AKC does not differentiate the sexes when considering size, but recognizes three different sizes: toys (9 to 12 inches [22.9–30.5 cm] inclusive), miniatures (over 12 up to 15 inches [30.5–38.1 cm]), and standards (over 15 up to 19 inches [38.1–48.3 cm]). Unlike the UKC, the AKC disqualifies dogs not meeting these height requirements.

The two standards describe ideal dogs having slightly different body proportions, with the UKC describing a basically square-bodied dog and the AKC describing one slightly longer than tall. The AKC standard is more explicit in its descriptions of pastern slope, muzzle proportions, toe shape, and pigment, specifically calling for

Standard Definitions

Withers: Highest point of the shoulder.

Stop: Transition point from forehead to muzzle, as viewed in profile.

Scissors bite: The back surface of the top incisors meet the front surface of the bottom incisors when the mouth is closed.

Topline: The line from the neck to the tail, viewed in silhouette.

Angulated: Refers to the angles formed between the shoulder blade and the humerus in the forequarters, and the pelvis, thigh, and knee in the rearquarters. Well-angulated requires these angles to be close to 90 degrees.

Point of hock: Anatomical correlate to the human heel.

Coupled: Area between the rib cage and the rearquarters.

Trot: Gait where diagonal legs move in unison.

Pace: Gait where legs on the same side of the body move in unison.

white toenails and dark footpads. It also states that tear stains (unless severe) should not be faulted.

A note about nose color: Like many breeds, many Eskies will get a "winter nose", meaning that the nose pigment gets lighter during the winter months.

The AKC Standard

The following is a reprint of the official standard for the American Eskimo dog. It was submitted by the American Eskimo Dog Club of America and approved by the Board of Directors of the American Kennel Club.

General Appearance

The American Eskimo dog, a loving companion dog, presents a picture of strength and agility, alertness and beauty. It is a small to medium-size Nordic type dog, always white, or white with biscuit cream. The

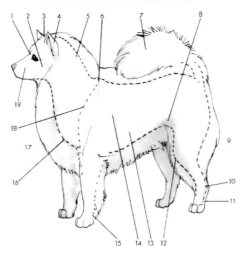

The surface anatomy of the American Eskimo dog: 1. stop 2. cheek 3. skull 4. ear 5. neck 6. withers 7. tail 8. loin 9. hindquarters 10. hock 11. rear pastern 12. stifle 13. rib cage 14. brisket 15. front pastern 16. chest 17. forequarters 18. shoulder 19. muzzle.

American Eskimo dog is compactly built and well balanced, with good substance, and an alert, smooth gait. The face is Nordic type with erect triangular shaped ears, and distinctive black points (lips, nose, and eye rims). The white double coat consists of a short, dense undercoat, with a longer guard hair growing through it forming the outer coat, which is straight with no curl or wave. The coat is thicker and longer around the neck and chest forming a lion-like ruff, which is more noticeable on dogs than on bitches. The rump and hind legs down to the hocks are also covered with thicker, longer hair forming the characteristic breeches. The richly plumed tail is carried loosely on the back.

Size, Proportion, Substance

Size. There are three separate size divisions of the American Eskimo dog (all measurements are heights at withers) Toy, 9 inches to and including 12 inches; Miniature, over 12 inches to and including 15 inches; and Standard over 15 inches to and including 19 inches. There is no preference for size within each division. Disqualification: Under 9 inches or over 19 inches.

Proportion. Length of back from point of shoulder to point of buttocks is slightly greater than height at withers, an approximate 1.1 to 1 ratio.

Substance. The American Eskimo dog is strong and compactly built with adequate bone.

Head

Expression is keen, intelligent, and alert. *Eyes* are not fully round, but slightly oval. They should be well set apart, and not slanted, prominent or bulging. Tear stain, unless severe, is not to be faulted. Presence of tear stain should not outweigh consideration of type, structure, or temperament. Dark to medium brown is the preferred eye color. Eye rims are black to dark brown. Eyelashes are white. Faults: amber eye color or pink eye rims. Disqualification: Blue eyes.

Ears should conform to head size and be triangular, slightly blunt-tipped, held erect, set on high yet well apart, and blend softly with the head.

Skull is slightly crowned and softly wedge-shaped, with widest breadth between the ears. The stop is well defined, although not abrupt. The *muzzle* is broad, with length not exceeding the length of the skull, although it may be slightly shorter. *Nose* pigment is black to dark brown. *Lips* are thin and tight, black to dark brown in color. Faults: pink nose pigment or pink lip pigment. The *jaw* should be strong with a full complement of close fitting teeth. The *bite* is scissors, or pincer.

Neck, Topline, Body

The *neck* is carried proudly erect, well set on, medium in length, and in a strong graceful arch. The *topline* is level. The *body* of the American Eskimo dog is strong and compact, but not cobby. The chest is deep and broad with well-sprung ribs. Depth of chest extends approximately to point of elbows. Slight tuck-up of belly just behind the ribs. The back is straight, broad, level, and muscular. The loin is strong and well-muscled. The American Eskimo dog is neither too long nor too short coupled. The *tail* is set moderately high and reaches approximately to the point of hock when down. It is carried loosely on the back, although it may be dropped when at rest.

Forequarters

Forequarters are well angulated. The shoulder is firmly set and has adequate muscle but is not overdeveloped. The shoulder blades are well laid back and slant 45° with the horizontal. At the point of shoulder, the shoulder blade forms an approximate

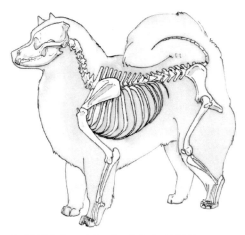

An Eskie's foundation is vitally important. The interaction of bones and muscle enable the properly built and maintained dog to run and jump with minimal effort.

right angle with the upper arm. The legs are parallel and straight to the pasterns. The pasterns are strong and flexible with a slant of about 20°. Length of leg in proportion to the body.

The musculature of the American Eskimo dog should be well developed. In a well-conditioned dog, the major muscle groups of the thigh, upper arm, and loin should be able to be felt beneath the coat.

This dog illustrates many of the points described in the official breed standard.

Dewclaws on the front legs may be removed at the owner's discretion; if present, they are not to be faulted. Feet are oval, compact, tightly knit and well padded with hair. Toes are well arched. Pads are black to dark brown, tough and deeply cushioned. Toenails are white.

Hindquarters

Hindquarters are well angulated. The lay of the pelvis is approximately 30° to the horizontal. The upper thighs are well developed. Stifles are well bent. Hock joints are well let down and firm. The rear pasterns are straight. Legs are parallel from the rear and turn neither in nor out. Feet are as described for the front legs. Dewclaws are not present on the hind legs.

Coat

The American Eskimo dog has a standoff, double coat consisting of a dense undercoat and a longer coat of guard hair growing through it to form the outer coat. It is straight with no curl or wave. There is a pronounced ruff around the neck which is more noticeable on dogs than bitches. Outer part of the ear should be well covered with short, smooth hair, with longer tufts of hair growing in front of ear openings. Hair on muzzle should be short and smooth. The backs of the front legs should be well feathered, as are the rear legs down to the hock. The tail is covered profusely with long hair. *There is to be no trimming of the whiskers or body coat and such trimming will be severely*

This beautifully groomed Eskie anxiously awaits its turn in the show ring.

penalized. The only permissible trimming is to neaten the feet and the backs of the rear pasterns.

Color
Pure white is the preferred color, although white with biscuit cream is permissible. Presence of biscuit cream should not outweigh consideration of type, structure, or temperament. The skin of the American Eskimo dog is pink or grey. Disqualification: Any color other than white or biscuit cream.

Gait
The American Eskimo dog shall trot, not pace. The gait is agile, bold, well balanced, and frictionless, with good forequarter reach and good hindquarter drive. As speed increases, the American Eskimo dog will single track with the legs converging toward the centerline of gravity while the back remains firm, strong, and level.

Temperament
The American Eskimo dog is intelligent, alert, and friendly, although slightly conservative. It is never overly shy nor aggressive, and such dogs are to be severely penalized in the show ring. At home it is an excellent watchdog, sounding a warning bark to announce the arrival of any stranger. It is protective of its home and family, although it does not threaten to bite or attack people. The American Eskimo dog learns new tasks quickly and is eager to please.

Disqualifications
Any color other than white or biscuit cream.
Blue eyes.
Height under 9″ or over 19″.

Breeding Your American Eskimo Dog

Is This Really Such a Good Idea?

It is only natural to consider the prospect of breeding your beautiful, wonderful, intelligent, one in a million Eskimo dog. But you should consider it long and hard, and then think some more. When you contacted breeders about acquiring your puppy, it may have seemed to you that it was indeed a seller's market; after all, if they were responsible breeders, they probably made it clear that they would not sell to you unless you met certain criteria, and they may have even had a waiting list for their puppies. You also probably had to pay a fair amount of money for your puppy, and it may seem logical that if you could multiply that by the number of pups in a litter, you would not only have recouped your investment but would have some extra pocket money. Think again. Breeders with waiting lists are usually those who have worked for years to achieve a reputation of having superior stock. Although your dog may be the exemplar of the Eskie standard in your eyes, it may instead just be the proof that love is blind. You need objective confirmation of her quality by earning titles attesting to her superiority. Don't breed your bitch unless you have a waiting list of several homes, each just as good as your own.

There are more reasons *not* to breed a litter than there are to breed one:

• A spayed female is less likely to develop breast cancer and a number of other hormone-related diseases.

• There is definite discomfort and a certain amount of danger to the bitch when whelping a litter. Watching a litter be born is not a good way to teach the children the miracle of life; there are too many things that can go wrong.

• A litter is expensive! Stud fee, prenatal care, whelping complications, supplemental feeding, puppy food, vaccinations, advertising, and a staggering investment of time and energy are all involved.

• Finding responsible buyers is very difficult, and you may end up feeling like the warden at a home for delinquent cotton balls.

• There are many more purebred Eskimo dogs in the world than there are good homes for them. The puppy you sell to a less than perfect buyer may end up neglected or discarded, or used to produce puppies to sell to even less desirable homes. Millions of purebreds are euthanized each year at pounds.

Then why on earth do people breed dogs at all? Ethical and knowledgeable breeders seldom do. They breed a litter only after studying the breed standard, studying pedigrees, and studying individual dogs to find the most advantageous match of conformation, temperament, and health, then proving the worth of both prospective parents through competitions, and then finding a number of responsible buyers. They have money set aside for prenatal and postnatal care, and emergency funds and vacation time available for whelping or post whelping complications. They have the commitment to keep every single puppy born for the rest of its life should good homes not be available or should they ever have to be returned. And they worry a lot. Is it any wonder that some of the best breeders breed the least? When they do breed, it is because they love the American Eskimo dog, and they believe that their puppies could be a worthwhile addition not only to the breed, but to somebody's life.

Dating, Mating, and Waiting

If you have decided that you are willing to take on the responsibility of being an ethical breeder of the American Eskimo dog, and your female is in fact worthy of being bred, and you do in fact have puppy buyers with deposits, then you need to choose the prospective father of your new puppies with great care. Be honest with yourself about your Eskie bitch's shortcomings, and make these areas a priority in choosing a stud. At the same time, write down the aspects of your bitch (and of Eskies in general) that are most important to you, and that you do not wish to sacrifice at any cost. Keep these traits in mind when you evaluate studs, their parents, and their offspring. Chances are you have just shortened your list of potential suitors drastically.

The Pedigree

Now the pedigree becomes an important tool. Perhaps one of the potential studs is your bitch's brother.

Reminder: the UKC frowns upon the mating of close relatives: father to daughter, mother to son, or brother to sister.

Inbreeding: Inbreeding more technically refers to a system of mating that makes it more likely that an offspring will inherit identical copies of the same gene from both its mother and father.

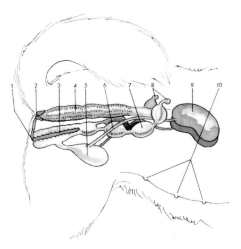

The internal organs of the female: 1. vulva 2. anus 3. vagina 4. rectum 5. bladder 6. ureter 7. developing embryo 8. ovaries 9. kidney 10. mammary glands.

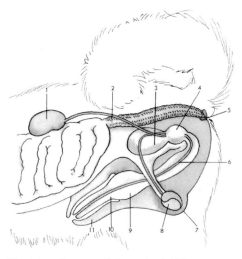

The internal organs of the male: 1. kidneys 2. rectum 3. bladder 4. prostate 5. anus 6. urethra 7. scrotum 8. testes 9. bulb 10. penis 11. sheath.

A proud mother nurses her new litter, which was the result of careful planning and meticulous care.

Future champions.

The problem with inbreeding lies in the fact that the majority of serious hereditary defects are recessive in nature, meaning that two identical copies of the gene for that defect must be inherited for the trait to be expressed—exactly what inbreeding promotes! In general, unless there is a specific reason to, and you have a firm grasp of the genetic principles involved, such inbreeding is not advisable.

Linebreeding: Look again at the proposed pedigree of the union. Is there one name that appears over and over? Breeding with a concerted effort to intensify the genetic influence of a particular individual is called linebreeding; such breeding will also be somewhat inbred, and carries the same caveat (though usually to a lesser degree) as does inbreeding. Never try to linebreed on a name only; it is meaningless unless you know what specific traits the wonder dog possessed that would make you want to take the chances involved in inbreeding and linebreeding.

Outcrossing: Are there no common names in the pedigree? Then your breeding will be an outcross. An outcross is generally the safest way to go, but has the shortcoming that the results are less predictable.

Remember, the pedigree is more than just a list of strange names that you can trot out to impress your friends. It is a valuable tool that lets you know how your litter is likely to look. If you are serious about producing quality Eskies you should do everything you can to obtain pictures or descriptions to go with these names. The pedigree is a history of breeding decisions. With study, work, and luck, perhaps your litter will be a decision that will one day be looked upon as brilliant!

Prenuptials
The chances of the ideal stud for your bitch living down the street, or being owned by a co-worker, are remote. A responsible stud owner will have proven the stud by earning titles,

will have complete records and photos of other litters the stud has produced, and will insist that your bitch and your facilities be adequate before accepting her for breeding. Make arrangements well before your female comes into season. Ask for a written contract that spells out what fees will be due and when, what arrangements for your bitch's housing will be made, and what will happen if no (or only one) puppy is born.

Both dogs to be bred should have a blood test for canine brucellosis, a primarily (but not exclusively) sexually transmitted disease with devastating effects on fertility. The female should also have a prebreeding checkup to ensure that she is in good health and does not have any abnormalities that would make whelping difficult. Eskie females should not be bred on their first season or before the age of two years.

Monitor her closely for signs of "heat" (estrus). Most dogs are breedable for several days sometime between the eighth and eighteenth day of estrus, although earlier and later alliances have been known to result in pregnancy. Your veterinarian can also monitor her progress by microscopic examination of vaginal smears or blood tests. As she approaches her receptive stage, she will tend to "flag" her tail, or cock it to the side when the male approaches or if you scratch around the base of her tail. Experienced stud dogs will not need calendars or microscopes; until that time they may court and strut and dance, but their attempts to mount are generally halfhearted.

Although the two suitors may dance and flirt, when it comes time for business the female may become frightened or aggressive, and it is best if she is held on-leash and possibly muzzled. The male may need some subtle guiding but too much interference may discourage him.

Upon intromission he will step from side to side, and then will want to jump off of her and turn by lifting one hind leg over her back, so that they can stand rear to rear. This "tie" is perfectly normal for dogs and will typically last from 10 to 30 minutes. Keep both of them cool and calm during this time. For optimal chances of conception, repeat this procedure every other day until she will no longer accept the male. Be sure to keep her away from other males during this time; dogs are not known for their fidelity!

Eating for Five?

Now you have two months to wait and plan. Gradually increase and change the expectant mother's food to a high-quality puppy food as time progresses. Keep her in shape, because a well-conditioned dog will have fewer problems whelping. At the end of the first month your veterinarian may be able to feel the developing puppies, but this is not always accurate. Two encouraging signs of pregnancy that will appear at around this same time are a clear mucous discharge from the vagina and enlarged, pink nipples. If at any time the discharge is not clear, seek veterinary attention at once.

False pregnancies: Many females are prone to false pregnancies: a condition in which the breasts become slightly enlarged and may even have some milk. Pronounced cases involving large amounts of milk production, weight gain, and even nesting behavior and the adoption of certain toys as "babies" may be unhealthy and should be checked by your veterinarian. Some can be so convincing that even experienced breeders have thought their bitch was in whelp until she failed to deliver puppies!

You should be counting the days from the first breeding carefully. Be sure that everything is ready at least one week before the big event.

Preparations

Where will the puppies be born? If you don't decide, you can be sure your mamma-to-be will choose the middle of your bed! But her own whelping box in a warm, quiet room is really best. This whelping box will be her den and the puppies' home for the first few weeks of their lives. It should be large enough for mother and babies to lie comfortably, but not so large that the babies can wander off and not find Mom. The sides should be high enough so that the young pups cannot get out, but low enough so that the mother can get over without scraping her now low-slung belly. A shelf or rail along the inside is a good idea to prevent the puppies from being trapped against the wall and crushed by the dam. Many people use children's plastic wading pools as whelping boxes for standards, or the bottom of a plastic cage for toy Eskies. In any case, the box should not be set directly on a cold floor, and should be lined with blank newspaper or preferably washable (formaldehyde-free) scatter rugs or sheets. Newspaper has the disadvantage of being slippery for puppies just learning to walk; also, colored sections can contain harmful chemicals, and the black ink turns white puppies gray! Introduce the expectant mother to the box well before whelping and encourage her to sleep in it.

Talk to your veterinarian or an experienced breeder about what to expect at whelping. If possible, arrange to have someone on call in case of any difficulty. You will need the following: rectal thermometer, many towels and washcloths, nasal aspirator, blunt-nose scissors, dental floss, heating pad or heat lamp, and a warm box for placing newborns in while awaiting the arrival of their siblings. Keep a hospital atmosphere in your delivery room; that is, everything that will come in contact with the newborns should be sterilized.

Several days before your Eskie's due date, clip the long hair from her belly, chest, and vulva. Then wash and thoroughly rinse these same areas.

The Big Day

Although 63 days is the average gestation time, there is some variability. But you can get about 12 hours advance notice by monitoring the prospective mother's temperature starting around the fifty-sixth day; when her temperature drops to about 98°F (36.7°C), make plans to stay home because labor is soon to follow! Warm the whelping box to 80°F (26.7°C), and prepare for a long night. She will become more restless, refuse to eat, and repeatedly demand to go out. Make her as comfortable as possible and do not let her go outside alone where she might have a puppy. The puppies are preceded by a water bag; once this has burst, the first puppy should be born soon. As each baby is born, help the mother clear its face so it can breathe; then you may wish to tie off the umbilical cord about 0.75 inch (19 mm) from the puppy with dental floss, and then cut the rest off with blunt-nose scissors. If you prefer, you can let the mother cut the cord, but watch to make sure she doesn't injure the pup. Each puppy should be followed by an afterbirth, which the dam will try to eat. Allow her to eat one or two as they contain important hormones affecting milk production, but eating too many will give her diarrhea. You must count the placentas to make absolutely sure that none was retained in her; retained placentas can cause serious infection. Dry the puppy and place it on the mother's nipple to

These contented puppies nap after snacking.

Use a large flat shallow bowl to feed young puppies. If desired, place a smaller bowl upside down in the middle of the larger bowl to keep the food near the edges. Place the larger bowl on paper, and be prepared to wipe the puppies (and surroundings) clean afterward.

nurse. When she begins to strain to produce the next puppy, remove the first one to a safe box warmed to 90°F (32.2°C). If at any time the mother strains without producing a puppy for over 20 minutes, call your veterinarian. Puppies can become stuck in the birth canal and a cesarean section may be necessary in order to save the rest of the litter and sometimes the dam. Eskie mothers are relatively easy whelpers, but all dogs can have problems. The smaller toy Eskies may have puppies that are too large to be born naturally, especially if they have been bred to a larger male. You got her into this mess; it's your duty to get her out.

These two babies are making friends with each other.

The American Eskimo Dog Club of America Code of Ethics

As a member of the AEDCA, I agree to abide by the following rules:

1. To give my dogs proper health care through timely vaccinations, worming, and veterinary care when needed.

2. To plan each litter with care, and breed only those dogs of sound body and mind. These dogs will be free of disqualifying and major faults as outlined in the American Eskimo Breed Standard.

3. To keep all official registration papers and contracts in accordance with AKC rules and regulations.

4. To never sell any puppies to pet stores or commercial dog brokers, or to give puppies or dogs to be used in any kind of promotional activities, such as a prize in a raffle.

5. To get a fair price for my puppies and dogs, because I have invested time and money to insure the quality of my pets or show dogs, and I cannot afford to sell them at cheap prices.

6. To be fair in my dealings with the public and prospective buyers regarding my dog and the American Eskimo breed.

Care of the Mother and Puppies

It is not always easy to tell when the last baby is born. If you have any doubts, have your veterinarian check her (you should bring her and the puppies for a post birth check the next day anyway). Usually the new mother will want to clean her puppies and fall asleep after her exhausting ordeal. Her once shiny white britches will be a mess and you should wipe them off and thoroughly dry her so that she will not chill the newborns. Besides letting her rest, your most important job now is to keep the babies warm. Puppies cannot regulate their body temperature, and chilling can quickly result in death. Whenever the dam must leave them, be sure that they are not in a draft. Use a heat lamp or heating pad to maintain their environment at 85 to 90°F (29.4°C) for the first week, 80°F (26.7°C) for the second week, and 75°F (23.9°C) for the third and fourth weeks. Never feed a chilled puppy, except for a few drops of sugar water. You should weigh each puppy daily to make sure that it is gaining weight.

The first few weeks Mom does most of the work, but you still must tidy the bedding and be sure that she is getting enough of her puppy food diet. Check to make sure that her breasts do not become hard and swollen or painful, which could indicate mastitis. Although she will continue to have a bloody discharge for a week or two after the birth, any signs of infection or foul odor associated with it is cause for immediate concern.

Small dams, such as toy Eskies, may be prone to eclampsia, a life-threatening condition arising when lactation demands are high. Early signs are nervousness, twitching, and a stiff gait, followed by fever and convulsions. Remove the puppies and get her to the emergency veterinarian at once, day or night.

Eskimo puppies are born with pink pigmentation, which gradually turns dark beginning a few days after birth. Talk to your veterinarian about the pros and cons of dewclaw removal (rear dewclaws, if present, should always be removed). If you opt to have this done, it should be performed by three days of age. The puppies' eyes will open starting around ten days of age, and their ears around two weeks. This age marks the beginning of rapid mental and physical growth. They will attempt to walk at two weeks of age. Be sure to give them solid footing (*not* slippery newspaper!). At around three weeks, you can introduce them to food: baby food or baby cereal or dry dog food mixed with water and put through the blender is a good starter. They may lick it off your finger or you may have to put their noses in it. No matter what technique you use, be prepared to declare the feeding arena a major disaster area by the time the meal is over. Puppies seem to think they can best eat with their feet!

Locating the Right New Eskie Owner

Young puppies are irresistible, and your house may become the newest tourist attraction on the block. Don't let the puppies be overhandled, and don't allow the mother to become stressed by onlookers. Talk to your veterinarian about your puppies' vaccination schedule and visitors, because they could bring contagious diseases with them. After about six weeks of age, it is important that the puppies meet people so that they are well socialized, but this does not mean that they need to be exposed to a constant stream of new faces. The puppies will be old enough to go to new homes at eight weeks of age, so you need to start preparing for potential new owners to visit.

As the puppies get older and make progressively larger messes, you may wonder whatever happened to your friends who were just dying to have one of Snopuff's babies. Now you may be faced with getting calls from strangers interested in buying these babies you've become so attached to. Remember the questions you asked yourself about whether the Eskie was the dog for you? You must ask these prospective owners how they plan to care for their puppy, what their long-term plans are for the puppy, and why they want an Eskimo dog at all. One breeder relates that she evaluates prospective buyers by whether, if she had to give up the mother dog, she could be confident that this person would be a good home for her.

Sometimes in desperation you may be tempted to give your babies away. Don't. There are unethical people in the world who scour the classifieds for free animals, and who have plans for these animals that don't include their surviving very long. People take better care of something in which they have an investment, so don't cheapen your puppies' lives.

You are responsible for bringing these little defenseless lives into the world. You are responsible for deciding whom you will entrust to care for them. A wrong decision on your part can condemn a puppy to a life of cruelty, neglect, or misuse. A right decision can mean matching a puppy and owner who will form a wonderful lifelong relationship. You are responsible for each trusting bundle of love, and you are responsible for each for the rest of their lives.

This pup's fate will depend upon the ability of its breeder to settle for only the best of homes for it.

Useful Addresses and Literature

International Kennel Clubs

American Kennel Club
   51 Madison Avenue
   New York, NY 10038
   212-696-8200

For registration information:
   American Kennel Club
   5580 Centerview Drive
   Raleigh, NC 27606
   919-233-9767

United Kennel club
   100 East Kilgore Road
   Kalamazoo, MI 49001-5598
   616-343-9020

National Breed Clubs

American Eskimo Dog Club of
   America (AKC)*
   Carolyn Jester
   Route 3, Box 211B
   Stroud, OK 74079

National American Eskimo Dog
   Association (UKC)*
   Helen Clark
   3863 McElhaney Road SE
   Sublimity, OR 97385

American Eskimo Dog Club Rescue*
   Jamie Johnson
   919-479-5154

*This address or phone number may
   change with the election of new officers.
   The current listing can be obtained by
   contacting the American Kennel Club.

Books

Benyon, Barbara. *The Complete
   American Eskimo: A Special
   Kind of Companion.* Macmillan
   Publishing, 1990.

Hofman, Nancy J. and Cathy J.
   Flamholtz. *The American
   Eskimo.* OTR Publications,
   1989.

Periodicals

Dog Fancy
   P.O. Box 53264
   Boulder, CO 80322
   303-786-7306

Dog World
   29 North Wacker Drive
   Chicago, IL 60606
   312-726-2802

National Lost-Pet Registries

Tattoo-based Registries

National Dog Registry
   P.O. Box 118
   Woodstock, NY 12498-0116

Tattoo-A-Pet
   1625 Emmons Avenue
   Brooklyn, NY 11235
   800-TATTOOS (828-8667)
   or 800-828-8007

I.D. Pet
   74 Hoyt Street
   Darien, CT 06820
   800-243-9147

Centralized Tattoo Registry
Information
15870 Allen Road
Taylor, MI 48180
313-285-6311

Microchip-based Registry
Info Pet Identification Systems
517 West Travelers Trail
Minneapolis, MN 55337
800-INFOPET (463-6738)

No Tatto or Microchip Required
Petfinders
368 High Street
Athol, NY 12810
800-223-4747

Animal Protection Organizations
American Humane Association
P.O. Box 1266
Denver, CO 80201
(303) 695-0811

American Society for the Prevention of
Cruelty to Animals
441 East 92nd Street
New York, NY 10128
212-876-7700

Friends of Animals
P.O. Box 1244
Norwalk, CT 06856

For information about FoA's low-cost
neutering-and-spaying program call:
800-631-2212

The Fund for Animals
200 West 57th Street
New York, NY 10019
212-246-2096

The Humane Society of the United
States
2100 L Street, NW
Washington, DC 20037
202-452-1100

Index